HOW TO TALK TO YOUR BABY

DOROTHY P. DOUGHERTY

AVERY PUBLISHING GROUP

Garden City Park • New York

Text Illustrator: John Wincek
Cover Designer: Phaedra Mastrocola
  and Oscar Maldonado
Typesetter: Liz Johnson and Gary Rosenberg
In-House Editor: Elaine Will Sparber

Avery Publishing Group
120 Old Broadway
Garden City Park, NY 11040
1–800–548–5757
www.averypublishing.com

Permission Credits

Table 2.1 on page 9 is from Laliberte, Richard, "Parents Report," *Parents Magazine,* Vol. 72, No. 9 (September 1997). Copyright © 1997 Gruner & Jahr USA Publishing. Reprinted from *Parents Magazine* by permission.

The list of "Songs, Poems, and Fingerplays" on page 19 is from *Scholastic Parent & Child,* November/December 1993. Reprinted from *Scholastic Parent & Child* by permission.

Publisher's Cataloging-in-Publication

Dougherty, Dorothy P.
      How to talk to your baby/Dorothy P.
   Dougherty. — 1st ed.
      p. cm.
      Includes bibliographical references and index.
      ISBN: 0-89529-932-1

      1. Interpersonal communication in infants.
   2. Language acquisition—Parent participation.
   3. Language arts (Early childhood) I. Title.

BF720.C65.D68 1999   155.42′236
                                                                  QBI99-1003

Printed in the United States of America

10   9   8   7   6   5   4   3   2   1

Contents

I dedicate this book to my father,
who through his words and actions
always encouraged me to laugh,
enjoy life, and strive to achieve.

Acknowledgments

I am grateful to my husband and best friend, Kevin, for his support, patience, and love throughout this project and my life. I am also grateful to my boys, Nick and Tom, who have taught me how wonderful it is to be a mother. Thanks to my mom and dad, who always encouraged me, not only with words, but also actions, to reach for the stars and keep trying. Thanks to my sisters, Marie Burton and Elaine Flatch; my brother and sister-in-law, Nick and Barbara Paglione; and my father-in-law, John Dougherty, for always offering me encouragement and support. Marie, a wonderful mother of three young boys, was always willing to listen and share "real-life" ideas.

Special thanks to my "running" friends, M.J. Perskie and Wendy Davy, for their endless ability to say the right thing and to listen on those cold winter mornings. Also, to my colleagues and friends, Pat Maletto and Carol Camburn, who freely shared their expertise, kindness, and humorous outlooks on life with me.

And, finally, I am indebted to the thousands of children and parents with whom I have worked over the years. Thank you for allowing me to share my "special gift" with all of you.

Foreword

Congratulations! If you are reading this book, it means that you intend to give your child the best start in life that you can. Your time has come. It is your turn to lay the foundation for your child and the future generations of your family. This is not a small task in this age when busy single parents and two-career couples are seeking ways to strengthen their family ties and stimulate their children while still meeting all the other obligations of their daily lives.

The same as your time, the time for this book has come. It is time for parents to be taught the techniques of early language stimulation that until now have been reserved for professionals. Chapter 1 reviews the latest explosion of research that supports early language stimulation. A subsequent chapter educates parents about normal language development. This should help parents relax and encourage them to pay attention to their child's daily communication as it develops. When parents and children pay such rapt attention to each other, bonding is given a boost.

The five techniques of language stimulation described in Chapters 3 through 9 are really ways of bonding with your child. From birth to three years of age, learning is play, and these techniques offer methods of joining in the fun rather than passively letting good teaching opportunities slip by. These methods do not exist in an emotional vacuum. Children love the interaction! Parents love the interaction! These techniques do more than stimulate language. They help guide the loving, close family bonds that humans desire.

Please use this book like a reference. Read it through once to learn the information and skills you need to start or continue stimulating your child. You will be surprised at the creative ways in which you'll use these techniques once you are aware of them. Then refer back to the book periodically to sharpen your skills. If you have a friend with a child, the two of you can share ideas.

Finally, a note about the author. Dorothy Dougherty has a genuine gift for helping people learn language. I've seen her help the adult victims of brain trauma, as well as thousands of preschool- and school-aged children who needed speech and language therapy. Dorothy and I raised two honor students, and I credit the language stimulation she gave them for much of their success. This book is the realization of Dorothy's dream to give the gift of language to you and your child.

Kevin R. Dougherty, PhD

Preface

Long before I received my master's degree in Speech and Language Pathology from the College of New Jersey in 1980, I knew I wanted to dedicate my life to helping children learn to talk. My younger brother's language development had been slower than normal, and, as a young girl, I had often found myself translating his mumbled words. By co-founding Atlantic Behavioral Care with my husband, Kevin R. Dougherty, PhD, a psychologist, I am able to help parents who need guidance in assisting their children's speech and language development, plus provide therapy to the children.

As a full-time working mother, I never had enough time to spend with my two boys when they were young. I often picked my children up at daycare and headed straight for the supermarket. Therefore, I enjoyed finding new ways to help my sons learn valuable language skills as I went about my daily activities. As my boys continue to pursue academic success, a rich language foundation has proven critical.

Recent scientific research suggests that during the first three years of life, parents can help "shape" their baby's brain and set the foundation for their life's learning. This is because, as we now know, the human brain is not fully developed at birth. As a baby absorbs new sights, textures, scents, and sounds, the connections in her brain that make learning possible multiply and become stronger. If a child does not use certain brain connections, or does not use them enough, the connections are simply shed, lost forever. Many of these connections involve language skills.

Research has shown that children's development of language is an important step in their ability to learn and think, and has a significant impact on their overall educational experience. If a child is unable to understand other people or to express her own thoughts and feelings, she may have difficulty developing relationships with other people, as well as good self-esteem, both of which, in turn, may cause her to become isolated from her peers.

Wouldn't you like to provide your child with the most stimulating environment possible for learning and using language? Simply surrounding your baby with conversation is not the answer. Instead, you must interact with your baby in relation to what is going on around you, and encourage your baby's desire to communicate with you. In *How to Talk to Your Baby*, you will learn how to put your *Thoughts* and *Actions* into words to enhance your baby's *Language* and *Knowledge* by using a system that incorporates five methods—naming, describing, comparing, explaining, and giving directions. After having used these methods for only a short time, many parents have said that routine activities became a special time of learning, interaction, and closeness with their babies.

How to Talk to Your Baby is not about how professionals can help children. Instead, it shows parents how to enhance their children's language and learning themselves. It is written in an introductory and non-technical manner. At the same time, it is a comprehensive presentation of valuable information.

It is important to stress that the purpose of *How to Talk to Your Baby* is not to "rush" your child's development. As we all know, the onset of language, more than any other skill, varies among children. Always remember how unique and special your child is. Research tells us that children display a lot of variation in when they say their first words, as well as in how many words they say at two years of age. However, if your baby receives a lot of stimulation during what researchers call the "window of opportunity"—the years from birth through age three—she may say more words sooner, develop a larger vocabulary, and even score higher on later intelligence tests.

Through the years, I have found that parents lack the information needed to determine if their children are developing speech and language skills as they should, and the knowledge of what to do if they seem to be having a problem. This lack of knowledge sometimes puts pressure on a family and fosters tension between family members. It is, therefore, another intention of this book to provide parents and caregivers with guidelines about the stages of language development and what most children do at certain ages. Please note, however, that this book is not meant to take the place of a professional consultation with a pediatrician or speech/language pathologist. If you have any concerns or questions about your child's speech and/or language development, please consult your pediatrician or a speech/language pathologist for advice and/or a referral to the appropriate specialist.

Can you really maximize your young child's language and learning? A review of current research plus my own experience with parents and children indicate *yes*! By creating a learning environment that is fun, loving, and nurturing, you can provide your baby with benefits that will last for the rest of her life.

This book was written for you. You are your child's first and most important teacher. You are ultimately responsible for teaching your baby how to communicate with the world.

A Word
About Gender

Your baby is certainly as likely to be a boy as a girl. However, the English language does not provide a genderless pronoun. Therefore, to avoid the use of the awkward "he/she" when referring to a child and still give equal time to both sexes, the masculine pronouns "he," "him," and "his" are used in the odd-numbered chapters, and the female pronouns "she," "her," and "hers" are used in the rest. This has been done in the interest of simplicity and clarity.

1

Language and Communication

How many times today have you used words to get what you want or need, to pass on information, to express your feelings, or to influence other people? The words you used were a part of the language spoken around you.

Language is a set of symbols used by people to send and receive messages. These symbols may consist of words, facial or hand expressions, or even smoke signals. Speaking, reading, writing, gesturing, listening, watching, and understanding all are parts of language. All the languages of the world are organized by rules that govern the use of their symbols. If you know the rules governing how the words or symbols of a certain language are arranged, you can communicate in that language using sentences you have never heard and understanding things you have never spoken.

Your communication with your baby begins at birth. He may use cries of pain and smiles of delight to talk to you. By responding to your baby's communications, you show him that you understand his messages. Of course, when your baby begins to use words, his messages will become more clear and personal. He will be able to tell you that he is hurt or that he loves you.

Communicating with others involves receiving and understanding messages, as well as formulating and sending messages. When we send a message to another person, we use expressive language. Talking is a type of expressive language that uses speech, or sounds, to send these messages. When we understand what is written, spoken, or seen, we use receptive language.

RECEPTIVE LANGUAGE

In order to understand what is written, heard, or seen, you must attach meanings to the words or images that you read, hear, or see. You attach these meanings when you listen to other people talk and relate their words to the objects, people, actions, and events around you. Your understanding of new words develops as you build on the words you already know. When people talk to you, you understand their messages by using your receptive language skills. These skills include not only the ability to understand other peoples' words, but also to hear the differences in sounds, recall what was said, and interpret tone of voice and gestures. All of us occasionally find ourselves involved in the kind of conversation in which you have no idea what the other person is saying. Sometimes, we ask the speaker to repeat the statement, and other times, we simply proclaim, "I don't know what you're talking about!" Think about how hard it is to have a meaningful dialogue when you are unable to understand the message.

Before young children can use words themselves, they must understand what other people are saying by connecting meanings to objects and actions. Researchers agree that the normal range for the onset of receptive language—that is, the normal age span during which children begin to understand words said to them—is six to nine months old, with the average age being about eight months old. Experts suggest that if you talk to your baby a lot, you can significantly speed up the development of his ability to understand new words. This is because children build their receptive language skills by listening to other people talking to them. Words are not learned in isolation, but as part of a flow of phrases and sentences.

 TALKING TIME

Following is an example of a young child using receptive language:

Adult: "Where is the book?"

Child using receptive language: Points to the book.

Adult: "Yes, that's the bunny book!"

EXPRESSIVE LANGUAGE

Expressive language is the way we express our thoughts and feelings, answer questions, and relate events. It includes not only choosing words that have the correct meanings to relay the message we want to send, but also the tone of voice, gestures, and rate of speech we use. Babies learn quickly that communicating is a powerful tool that brings many exciting results. They use crying, sounds, and gestures to communicate before they use words. The normal range for when children begin to use actual words is large—nine to twenty-four months old, with the average age being about fourteen months old.

 TALKING TIME

Following is an example of a young child using expressive language:

Adult: "Please pick up the book."

Child using expressive language: Picks up book. "My book."

Adult: "Thank you. This is your book about animals."

SPEECH

One way to send messages is to use speech. Speech is the sounds you make when you communicate a message verbally. Speech begins when air is exhaled from the lungs. First the air is passed from the lungs to the larynx, and then it is shaped into specific sounds by moving the tongue, lips, teeth, and palate. In infancy, children learn to control their mouths and airflow by coughing, burping, crying, and babbling. As they mature physically, they learn to move the mouth, lips, tongue, and hard and soft palates in the correct ways to make sounds that form syllables and words.

Children acquire speech sounds gradually, and in a sequence that begins at birth and may continue through the seventh year of life. Generally, children are able to make the following sounds by the ages indicated:

❒ Three to four years old—b, d, g, h, k, m, n, p, t, w, and vowels (a, e, i, o, u).

❒ Five to six years old—l, ch, sh, and l blends (for example, bl, kl, and sl).

❒ Seven years old—r, s, z, r blends (for example, br, dr, and kr), and s blends (for example, sl, sm, sn, and st).

It is normal for some children to need a lot of practice before they are able to make all the sounds of their language correctly.

LANGUAGE AND LEARNING

All humans, at all ages, want to feel safe, have their needs satisfied, and have relationships with other people. All of these things are possible if we know language. How and what we say is an important part of who we are. Our ability to understand and use language affects our success and happiness throughout life.

Research has shown that the development of language skills is an important step in the development of the ability to learn and think, and will have a significant impact on a child's overall educational experience.

What Is a Language Disorder?

A language disorder is a noticeable problem with understanding and/or expressing thoughts and ideas. Some language disorders have physical causes, such as hearing impairment or cerebral palsy. However, language disorders often exist without physical or known causes. After a complete evaluation, a speech/language pathologist, who diagnoses and treats communication problems, may determine that a child has a language disorder if his language skills are significantly behind those of his peers in certain language milestones.

Following are some of the characteristics of children who have a language disorder:

❑ A child with a language disorder may have difficulty understanding words. For example, he may not be able to understand that the big colorful round toy he plays with at the beach is a ball, and that the small round toy he tosses to Dad in the yard is also a ball.

❑ A child with a language disorder may rarely ask questions. He may let adults do most of the talking. When he answers questions, he may seldom add additional information. He may usually speak in short phrases and sentences.

❑ A child with a language disorder may have difficulty understanding and using concept words. These are the words that describe concepts

This is because language skills are necessary to learn many of the other skills essential to success in school. When a child enters school, he needs to be able to understand other people and to express himself orally in order to be successful at such new tasks as reading and writing. Experts believe this is because learning to read and write actually begins with oral language. Children learn to organize their thoughts and focus their ideas by talking about themselves and their experiences. Children who are good listeners and speakers may become strong readers and writers. Evidence suggests that children who are slow at learning to speak and understand language may also be slow at learning how letters represent sounds, and may be unable to make sense out of what they read. Parents are usually concerned with their children's reading more than they are with any other skill in school. This makes sense because, throughout life, to under-

---

such as position (in, on, under), time (first, before, after), quality (big, old, cold), and quantity (more, some, one).

❒ A child with a language disorder may not be able to understand questions, or follow directions or the conversations of other people. This may be because he understands only parts of messages or is unable to pick out the important words. For example, when such a child is asked where he lives, he may answer, "I have a dog."

❒ A child with a language disorder may not be able use correct words to express what he means. He may substitute different words with related meanings (for example, "cake" for "cupcake"); he may substitute similar-sounding words ("knock" for "knob"); he may substitute visually related words ("clock" for "watch"); talk around words ("something we eat on" for "table"); he may frequently say "thing" or "stuff" instead of the proper words; or he may often insert long pauses between words and sentences.

❒ A child with a language disorder may have difficulty learning the rules of grammar. He may eliminate small words such as "in" and "the," or use pronouns incorrectly. For example, he may say, "Me like candy," instead of "I like candy."

Language-disordered children may have one or a combination of these difficulties.

stand and gain knowledge about the world, reading is essential. Also, if children can't express their thoughts orally, they may have difficulty writing them on paper. Paul Menyuk, a professor of developmental studies and applied linguistics at Boston University, concluded through his research, "Children who have trouble reading often have underlying speech and language problems."

Think how quickly a young child becomes frustrated when he can't tell another child to return his toy, can't play a game because he is unable to follow the directions, or can't express why he is sorry. As you can see, language difficulties can interfere with a child's ability to develop relationships with other people, as well as with his development of good self-esteem. The lack of these may, in turn, cause him to become isolated from his peers.

What fosters a love of learning more than success? Many children enter kindergarten wide-eyed and ready to learn, but instead need to play "catch-up." This may be because they don't have the language skills necessary to succeed. (For a discussion of language disorders, see "What Is a Language Disorder?" on page 4.) *How to Talk to Your Baby* will help you cultivate your baby's language skills. Read it through, from beginning to end, to get an overview of language and the language skills, then refer to it as necessary for ideas and encouragement.

How to Talk to Your Baby is organized in a logical sequence and written in easy-to-understand language. In Chapter 2, you will learn how nature and nurture are intertwined when it comes to helping children reach their highest potential. By being aware of what is happening inside your baby's brain before he says his first word, you will hopefully enjoy each tiny miracle along the way.

In Chapters 3 through 8, you will learn how to create a language-rich environment and enhance your baby's learning. Illustrations and examples provide easy-to-understand and enjoyable explanations. In Chapter 9, you will learn how and when most children develop the different language skills. You will also find that this chapter offers brain-boosting tips and toys to enhance your child's learning at the different stages.

A special chapter, Chapter 10, will explain why "Joey" and other young children may not develop language skills as quickly as their peers. Parents who have any concerns about their child's development will learn how to seek professional assistance.

Rounding out the book is a "Parent Glossary," which provides definitions for key terms to help make your reading easier. An appendix provides a "Parent Worksheet" to help you plan the assistance you give your child, and a list of "Resources for Parents and Caregivers" that includes Federal agencies, private organizations, and websites designed to assist and support your efforts.

In the next chapter, we will discuss how babies' brains are equipped to learn any language in the world, and how the stimulation you provide your baby now will lay the groundwork for his future success.

2

How Babies
Learn to Talk

In order for a baby to learn to talk, certain physical and sensory conditions must exist. Physically, the child must have lungs for air power; vocal cords that vibrate and make sounds; a tongue, lips, and hard and soft palate to shape air into meaningful sounds; and a functioning brain to receive and send messages. The baby must be able to hear the words spoken to her, and to see and focus on objects and people to learn word labels. She must be aware of how things feel, especially around her mouth, to learn how to place her lips and tongue to make the different sounds. She must be able to organize and make sense out of what she sees, hears, touches, and tastes.

Many parents would say that their babies began to talk when they said their first word. However, in reality, children begin to prepare for that show-stopping moment while still in the womb. In this chapter, we will discuss some of the tiny miracles along the way to that first word.

A BABY'S MAGNIFICENT BRAIN

Even before a woman may know that she is expecting, the first of 100 billion brain cells begin to multiply frantically inside the tiny embryo she is carrying. This is because a baby's brain begins to develop nerve cells, or neurons, just three weeks after conception. These neurons will carry electrical messages through the baby's brain. At birth, some of these neurons have already been given a job, determined by the genes the baby received from her mother and father. These neurons are the ones that are hardwired to control the baby's breathing, heartbeat, body temperature, and reflexes, such as sucking.

We now know that a baby does not arrive in this world with a fully assembled brain. Beginning shortly after birth, a baby's brain begins to undergo magnificent changes. During the first years of life, it will actually double in weight and use twice as much energy as an adult brain. This is not because of new cell growth, but because of the trillions of connections, or pathways, that develop between the cells. These connections enable the baby to think and learn.

Babies simply do not receive enough genes from their mother and father to make all of these pure, unprogrammed connections work. Scientists now know that what a child sees, hears, touches, and feels before the age of three strengthens and shapes the trillions of finer connections that will work together to foster her learning throughout life. However, at different times during a baby's development, some of the pathways that have not been used and reinforced by learning experiences in the outside world may be shed and lost forever. If a baby is provided with a lot of stimulation, however, the connections are strengthened and may remain active forever.

Think of a baby's brain as a forest with many trails going through the thick brush. Like a baby's brain pathways, the trails that are frequently traveled are always ready for passage and remain ready forever. The trails that aren't used become overgrown with brush and then can never be used.

> *It is impossible to qualify how significant the role of early learning is, but it is clear that during the first year of life, many critical windows of opportunity open and close.*
> —Carla Shatz, PhD, professor of neurobiology
> at the University of California at Berkeley

TALKING AND A BABY'S BRAIN

Babies learn to talk by listening. Research tells us that the more words babies hear, the faster they learn to talk. This is because frequent daily exposure to words helps the brain pathways that foster language learning to develop more fully. However, only "live" language, not television, helps children develop language skills. Experts feel this is because children need to hear language in relation to what is happening around them or it just becomes noise. It must be delivered by an engaged human being, and the child must focus on the speaker and environment.

According to research conducted by Janellen Huttenlocher, the actual size of a toddler's vocabulary is strongly correlated with how much her mother talks to her. Dr. Huttenlocher found that at twenty months old, the children of chatty mothers averaged 131 more words than the children of mothers who didn't speak much. At two years of age, the gap more than doubled to 295 words. (See Table 2.1.)

Other researchers have found that talking to children a lot not only affects their vocabulary, but also their intelligence. Betty Hart, PhD, and Todd R. Risley, PhD, observed how parents interacted with their one- and two-year-old children. At age three, the ones who scored the highest on intelligence quotient (IQ) and language tests were the ones who had heard the greatest number of words at one and two. It makes sense that these experts found the talkative parents automatically used more descriptive words, asked more questions, and explained more, rather than simply saying "stop" and "no." In third grade, when these children were re-tested, the children of the chatty parents were still found to have greater language skills than the children whose parents did not talk as much.

Even though your baby may be surrounded by conversation from

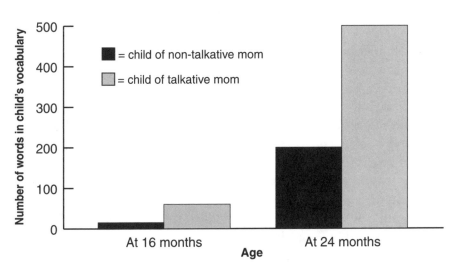

Table 2.1. Effect of parental chattiness on children's vocabulary.

Source: Laliberte, Richard, "Parents Report," Parents Magazine, Vol. 72, No. 9 (September 1997), page 50.

birth on, it is important that you talk directly to her long before she can talk back to you. You don't need to ask her a lot of questions or require her to respond. Your purpose is to build her understanding of language to help enhance her expression of language. Some experts have even said that talking and interacting with a baby early in life can actually make a difference between the baby having low-average communication skills and high- or above-average communication skills.

BEFORE THE FIRST WORD

As previously mentioned, before a baby says her first word, she must hear that word many times and understand its meaning. She also must be able to hear the differences between sounds in words, recognize where words begin and end, and understand how words are put together to form phrases and sentences in the language spoken around her. This is a complex task because, when we speak, we don't pause between each individual word, but rather, talk in a steady stream using the sounds that make up words.

Hearing the Differences Between Sounds

Children's language learning begins in the womb as they listen to the sound of their mother's voice for nine months. From the moment of birth, children can tell the difference between men's and women's voices. Within a week after birth, they develop a preference for their mother's voice over other voices, and soon afterwards, they begin to prefer their father's voice to other men's voices.

At first, infants respond only to the rhythm and melody of voices. However, remarkably, soon after birth, they begin to perceive the differences in the actual sounds that make up words. Researchers have found that four-month-old infants can hear the differences between every sound in every language. This is extremely difficult even for adults to do, since in each of the world's 6,000 languages, a different assortment of sounds is used to build words. However, by the age of ten months, an American baby surrounded by English-speaking adults has learned to tune out the sounds of the French language, for example, and concentrate more on the sounds of English. Researchers believe that babies, as they develop, don't lose the ability to hear the differences in sounds, but simply stop paying attention to the sounds they don't hear too often. This may allow them to concentrate on and learn the syllables and words of the language spoken by the people around them.

> *It was previously thought that language began when kids started talking to us at about one year of age. The new research shows that this is incorrect and that infants are mapping the sound structure of language in the first six to 12 months.*
> —Patricia Kuhl, PhD, professor of speech and hearing sciences
> at the University of Washington at Seattle

Recognizing Words

At around eight months of age, long before they know what most words mean, babies begin to unlock the mysteries of how their language puts sounds together to make syllables and words. Researchers believe this is due to their being accustomed to hearing certain combinations of sounds by the time they are seven months old. American babies living in English-speaking households become used to hearing combinations such as *t* and *r* (train trip), and *c* and *l* (clown, clean, clip). At the same time, they do not often hear combinations such as *db*, *gd*, or *ts* very often. Hearing certain combinations repeatedly allows babies to develop an ear for syllables. This makes the beginning and end of words less mysterious, even if the words themselves are not understood.

Children continue to learn about word boundaries and to develop an ear for the metrical or rhythmical patterns between them. In English, the first syllable of a word is often stressed (*DOG gy, MOM my, DAD dy*), particularly when speaking to young children. Researchers have found that children aged six to nine months old will suck more vigorously when they hear words with the first syllable accented, regardless of whether the words are read from a list or presented in the stream of normal talking. Researchers believe this tells us that babies less than a year old hear speech not as a blur, but as a series of meaningless words.

Understanding the Meanings of Words

By their first birthday, most children have begun to understand what different words mean. At first, children understand many more words than they can say. The MacArthur Communicative Development Inventories (CDIs) tell us that an average twelve-month-old child understands around 55 words, but might say 1 or 2. The average sixteen-month-old child understands about 170 words, but can say only about 25 of them.

According to Ellen Markman, a Stanford University psychologist, when children begin to say words, what they don't need to know is all of the meanings of every word in the language. This is because they start with three basic assumptions that help simplify what words mean. First, children figure out that labels refer to whole objects, not just a part or a quality of something. For example, they understand that the word "cup" refers to the whole item, not just the handle. Second, children assume that a word label does not refer to just one thing, but a class of things. This enables them to make generalizations, although not always correct ones. For example, an incorrect generalization that some children make is that, because a beach ball is a ball and a baseball is a ball, an orange is a ball. Third, children assume that anything with a name has only one name.

Understanding How Words Are Linked Together

Language is made up of words that are strung together. Children discover even before they start to put words together themselves that words can have different meanings depending on where they are located in sentences. For example, the sentence "Mom is calling Dad" has a different meaning than "Dad is calling Mom." Linguists believe that this enables children to analyze grammar and put words together in a way that can be understood by the people around them. Roughly 90 percent of the sentences that a three-year-old says are grammatically correct. But how do babies learn all of the abstract rules of grammar so quickly?

Noam Chomsky, a linguist with the Massachusetts Institute of Technology, revealed in the 1950s that children can't possibly learn all the rules and structures of language simply by listening to other people and repeating what they hear. Chomsky realized that in all the languages in the world, sentences are built using noun phrases ("the happy boy") and verb phrases ("ran home"). Researchers believe that, rather than memorizing millions of sentences, children master recipes for noun phrases and verb phrases. They are able to do this because they are born knowing "universal grammar"—that is, the fundamental rules that are common to all languages. Linguists believe that, because babies come equipped with this software to analyze grammar, they can apply these rules to the speech they hear without having to understand why or how it works. Studies show that toddlers who never heard of grammar can identify noun and verb phrases.

The mistakes children usually make are because they follow the rules of grammar too closely and don't account for the irregularities in a language. It is not uncommon to hear a young child say things such as: "The dog runned away." "I have two foots." "This one is gooder."

NATURE AND NURTURE

Researchers have a long way to go before they can determine exactly how babies learn to talk. Most scientists agree that babies' brains are wired for this task. This is because most children, from all parts of the world, learn to speak and understand words at around the same age, and even follow the same stages of language development. We know that genes affect babies' intelligence, but parents' interest in and interactions with their children from the moment of birth is essential. This is because the most critical period in the development of babies' brains is from birth to age three.

Most researchers believe that children need stimulation, and they need it early. Some parents believe this means they should bombard their children with educational experiences and endless chatter. On the contrary, helping your child learn to talk can be fun and easy, and a part of your everyday routine. In the next chapter, we will learn how to create a loving, fun, and language-rich environment for a young child.

3

Creating a Language-Rich Environment

In the last chapter, we learned that the more the parents and other people speak to a child, the more words that child will acquire. All parents, no matter how busy they are, want their children to grow fully in each stage of development. In this chapter, we will explore ways in which you can interact with your child in daily situations to enhance his language skills and help him develop to his full potential. You will find hundreds of opportunities throughout the day to help your child learn to talk.

By following the suggestions in this chapter, and adding ideas of your own, you can create a language-rich environment for your child. Most of the suggestions are appropriate for children of all ages. If necessary, you can adapt them to meet the specific needs of your child. The language-rich environment you create will encourage your child to talk by giving him a reason to communicate. Relax, have fun, and enjoy helping your youngster learn.

TUNE INTO YOUR CHILD AND FOLLOW HIS LEAD

Researchers believe that it is very important not to push your child, but rather, to follow his lead. Be affectionate with your child and responsive to his actions. This will make him feel important and confirm his sense of self. Your child will know from your caring attention that you are special, too. His trust will enable you to play an active role in his future learning.

Keep talking and playing with your child as long as he listens. A baby will smile and tell you with body language and eye contact that he is engaged in the activity. Stop when he signals that he has had enough. He may cry, turn his head away, or even arch his back. As your child begins to communicate with you, focus on words and objects that are central to his life or on which he is focusing at the moment. For example, if he is pointing at a squirrel running up a tree, don't start talking about the dog across the street. Talk about the squirrel: "It's a squirrel. Look at his bushy tail. He is going up the tree."

KNOW WHAT TO EXPECT FROM YOUR CHILD

Many parents compare their child's language development to that of their other children or other children in the neighborhood. However, there is a lot of variation in what is considered normal in this area, especially in a baby's second year of life. Just as children mature physically at different rates, they develop language at different rates. Since both expecting too much and too little can be harmful, it is important to know if your child is developing and progressing in all areas at an acceptable rate. A discussion of how and when most children develop speech and language skills is presented in Chapter 9, "The Stages of Language Development." If you have any concerns or questions about your child's development, consult your pediatrician or a speech/language pathologist.

BE A GOOD LISTENER

Initially, your relationship with your baby is one-sided. You talk, he listens. However, beginning shortly after birth, he begins to express himself with sounds and facial expressions. When he coos and babbles, just be quiet and listen. Stop what you are doing, and make eye contact. Stand close to your child, and bend down to his eye level. Then respond. Repeat what he says, or use words that tell him you approve of his talking and understand his message: "Oh, is that right?" Being a good listener teaches your child a fundamental part of all communication—taking turns.

When your toddler rushes in, obviously anxious to tell you something very important, set a good example. If possible, stop what you are doing, and give him your attention. Most children, as well as adults, are more willing to communicate when they are looking at the other person's face, rather than the person's back or side. By giving your child your undivided attention, you will show him how to listen when someone has something important to say.

BE A GOOD MODEL

Experts believe that you should not use or encourage "baby talk." Speak clearly, naturally, and, most important of all, correctly. For example, don't say: "You want your baba! Me so hungry." Children learn the language that they hear. Before your baby speaks, he will listen to everything you say and how you say it. When he starts to talk, he will imitate the word patterns he has been hearing. Instead, try this: "You want your bottle. You are so hungry!" Modeling the correct way to speak will help your child learn the correct way to speak.

Refer to yourself and other people using the proper pronouns. Don't say: "Mommy is so proud of you." Instead, say: "I am so proud of you." Your child will learn to use pronouns, such as "I," "he," and "she," by listening to you use these words correctly.

HELP YOUR CHILD DEVELOP LISTENING SKILLS

Children must listen to learn, and learn to listen. Learning how to follow directions is one way children learn to listen. To help your child understand the directions you give him, point and use other gestures. Your child will probably listen and understand only when you speak at his level of understanding.

One- and two-year-old children respond to simple one-step directions. For example, don't say: "Show me the apple near the brown cow." Instead, say: "Show me the cow," or "Show me the apple."

Two- and three-year-old children can follow one-step directions that contain concept words, such as "little" or "big." For example, they should be able to understand directions such as, "Bring me the little cup." They can also follow two-step directions, such as, "Get your shoes and bring them to me."

Hearing the differences between sounds, or auditory discrimination, is a critical link to reading. Begin early, and give your child experience listening to many different sounds. Comment on the sounds around you: "Listen to the clock ticking." Or ask: "Do you hear that airplane? It is loud." Talk about the sounds your child makes when he splashes in the tub, claps his hands, and stamps his feet. Bang pots with spoons, or drop blocks into different empty containers. Plastic, metal, and cardboard containers all make different sounds.

PLAY MUSIC, SING SONGS, AND RECITE NURSERY RHYMES

Moms all over the world instinctively know that singing soothes a fussy baby like nothing else. Psychologists feel that music benefits babies beginning in the earliest months of life, when the brain connections are forming. Some experts have stated that, by exposing a baby to music, parents enhance his ability to understand information and stimulate his language development. Scientific evidence suggests that children who listen to classical music, such as Mozart, as infants tend to score higher on IQ tests as preschoolers. Music helps babies develop good listening skills by enhancing their abilities to hear the differences in sounds and to repeat words they hear. Experts believe this is because babies use the same part of the brain to organize music and language into understandable segments.

When you play music for your baby, sing, dance, and laugh along. Show your enjoyment, and be part of the action. Although your baby is unique and may enjoy many different kinds of music, some experts feel that newborns are best comforted by quiet, soothing music, including lullabies, love ballads, gentle blues songs, and folk songs. When your baby sits on your lap, he may enjoy singing and listening to more upbeat songs, such as "Row Row Row Your Boat," "Itsy Bitsy Spider," and "Twinkle, Twinkle Little Star." Many of these songs have gestures that go with the lyrics. For crawlers and walkers, experts recommend songs about animals, body parts, and familiar routines, such as "Wheels on the Bus." Older babies may also enjoy bluegrass, Latin Renaissance, and dance music.

"Pat-a-Cake" and other nursery rhymes offer more than just entertainment. They are one of the earliest forms of communication that a child learns, and experts feel that they may benefit a child's growth in many areas, including social and language development. Hearing rhymes helps children learn how the language flows and builds their vocabulary skills. They listen intently to the rhythms and inflections, which also helps them develop listening skills. Toddlers enjoy rhymes that encourage participation. Keep your child physically involved whenever possible. For example, point to his body parts, touch his fingers and toes, and fall down at the end of "London Bridge."

For a list of recommended nursery rhymes, songs, poems, and fingerplays for your baby, see page 21.

Songs, Poems, and Fingerplays

As published in *Scholastic Parent & Child*, the following songs, poems, and fingerplays are recommended for young children.

Infants to 18 Months

Nursery Rhymes and Songs:

"This Little Piggy Went to Market"
"Here We Go Round the Mulberry Bush"
"Hush-A-Bye Baby" (can be sung when putting babies to sleep)
"One, Two, Buckle My Shoe" (sing while dressing a baby)
"Pat-a-Cake" (when feeding a baby)
"What Can the Matter Be" (when a baby is crying)

Songs, Poems, and Fingerplays:

The Stretching Song

> We like to play this little game
> All curled up in a ball.
>
> And then we rise a little bit,
> But still we're very small.
>
> Finally, we stand up straight.
> But still that isn't all.
>
> For then we stretch on tippy toes
> And we are very tall.

Body Parts Game

> Touch your nose,
> Touch your chin,
> That's the way this game begins.
> Touch your eyes,
> Touch your knees,
> Now pretend you're going to sneeze.
> Touch your hair,
> Touch one ear,
> Touch your two red lips right here,
> Touch your elbows where they bend,
> That's the way this touch game ends.

18 to 24 Months

Songs, Poems, and Fingerplays:

Blow Up a Balloon

> Blow up a balloon,
> (Blow with fingers to mouth)
> Blow up a balloon,
> (With hands, show increase in balloon size)
> Blow and Blow and Blow;
> Tie in a knot.
> (Mimic action)
> Push in the air.
> (Mimic action)
> Where did my balloon go?
> (Look around)

Here Is a Ball

> Here is a ball,
> (Make small circle with two hands)
> And here is a ball;
> (Make it a little larger)
> And a great big ball I see.
> (Hold arms wide above head)
> Won't you help me count the balls?
> One, two, three!

2 to 3 Years

Rhymes:

"Old MacDonald"
"London Bridge"
"Eency Weency Spider"
"Here We Go Round the Mulberry Bush"

Songs, Poems, and Fingerplays:

If You're Happy and You Know It

If you're happy and you know it,
Clap your hands.

If you're happy and you know it,
Clap your hands.

If you're happy and you know it,
And you really want to show it,

If you're happy and you know it,
Clap your hands.

Rain Poem

All the rain is falling down.
(Fingers reach to sky and then to ground)
Falling, falling to the ground.
The wind goes swish right through the air, (Arms overhead)
And blow the rain 'round everywhere.
(Make blowing face)

Source: Scholastic Parent & Child, November/December 1993.

Even if you're no Pavarotti, your lullabies and jingles help your child's brain development.

—Edwin Kiester, Jr., and Sally Valente Kiester,
"You Can Raise Your Child's IQ," *Reader's Digest,* October 1996

ENCOURAGE QUIET SOLITUDE

Experts feel that a baby's brainpower can be enhanced not just with stimulation, but also by exploring the world on his own. Babies can figure

American Library Association's Suggested Book List for Young Readers

This Suggested Book List for Young Readers provides suggestions for books that you can introduce to children at different ages.* Although some of these books have been developed for a particular age, many are old favorites that can be enjoyed at any age.

 Birth Through Eight Months

The following books have simple rhymes and poems.

Big Fat Hen, by Keith Baker
Ten, Nine, Eight, by Molly Bang
Play Rhymes, by Marc Brown
Goodnight Moon, by Margaret Wise Brown
Tomie DePaola's Mother Goose, by Tomie DePaola
Eye Winker, Tom Tinker, Chin Chopper: 50 Musical Finger Plays, by Tom Glazer
Rosie's Walk, by Pat Hutchins
Read Aloud Rhymes for the Very Young, by Jack Prelutsky
Have You Seen My Duckling? by Nancy Tafuri
My First Mother Goose, by Rosemary Wells

* The U.S. Department of Education recommends that parents review this list and make their own decision on the suitability of the books for their children.

Eight Months Through Eighteen Months

These books are short with a little text and many rhymes. At this age children really enjoy holding cardboard books and turning pages.

Moon Bear, by Rank Asch
Will I Have a Friend? by Miriam Cohen
Corduroy, by Don Freeman
Where's Spot? by Eric Hill
Mama, Do You Love Me? by Barbara Joose
Peter's Chair, by Ezra Jack Keats
Pat the Bunny, by Dorothy Kunhardt
Clap Hands, by Helen Oxenbury
Seven Blind Mice, by Ed Young
"More, More, More", Said the Baby, by Vera Williams

 Eighteen Through Thirty-Six Months

These books have more text and an easy-to-follow story that moves along quickly.

The Little Red Hen, by Bryon Barton
Clifford the Big Red Dog, by Norman Bridwell
Wait Till the Moon Is Full, by Margaret Wise Brown
Stellaluna, by Jannell Cannon
The Very Hungry Caterpillar, by Eric Carle
Millions of Cats, by Wanda Gag
Chicka Chick Boom Boom, by Bill Martin Jr. and Lois Ehlert
Curious George, by H.A. Rey
The Cat in the Hat, by Dr. Suess
The Bunny Planet, by Rosemary Wells

This reading list was developed at the American Library Association (ALA) under the Born to Read Project, which builds partnerships between librarians and health care providers to reach out to new and expectant parents and help them raise children who are "born to read."

Source: America Reads Challenge: Ready Set Read for Caregivers: Early Childhood Language Activities for Children From Birth Through Age Five (Washington, DC: Corporation for National Service, U.S. Department of Education, and U.S. Department of Health and Human Services, 1997).

things out and solve problems without their parents making comments or directing them. Sometimes, children like to play with their parents nearby and available, and experts agree that this helps the development of their ability to learn. However, resist the urge to step in immediately if your child uses a toy or object in a safe, but strange or unique way. Wait until you see him becoming frustrated, then offer gentle guidance. Show him, and let him try again.

READ TO YOUR BABY

Experts agree that it is never too early to begin reading to a baby. Being held in your arms and listening to your voice is a pleasant activity for your baby. When you read a picture book, no matter how young your baby is, you will help to develop his visual, vocabulary, and listening skills. Storytime can also provide opportunities for emphasizing sounds, intonation patterns, and word meanings. By listening to your words, your baby will learn how to shape his babbles into words. Later, reading will help your baby grasp the idea that stories have a beginning, middle, and end. Waiting to see how a story continues or ends helps children develop good attention skills. Research tells us that the children who were read to by their parents come to school better prepared for learning. To help find appropriate books to read to your child, see the "American Library Association's Suggested Book List for Young Readers" on page 24.

PRAISE, PRAISE, AND PRAISE

Show your baby how excited you are when he smiles, imitates your mouth movements, or says new words. Praise your child for even the smallest accomplishment. Research has shown that this not only delights a child, but also actually reinforces the connections in his brain. If a baby's achievements are frequently met with no reaction or indifference, his brain circuits will not be strengthened, and he may become reluctant to try new things. Show your baby with smiles, hugs, and attention how much you enjoy talking with him. This will encourage him to talk to other people.

Even when you are very proud of your child's accomplishments, resist the temptation to have him "perform" in front of others, unless he enjoys doing so. Or, do the activity with him. For example, if you want him to count for Grandma, say the numbers with him.

RECOGNIZE AND CREATE LEARNING OPPORTUNITIES

Parents, of course, want to provide their children with many opportunities to learn new things. Going to a zoo, hands-on museum, and aquarium all provide your child with wonderful opportunities to learn about the world. However, these usually are not everyday excursions. Therefore, it is important that you learn to recognize the hundreds of opportunities that exist each day as you go about your routine activities with your child. Talking can and should be a part of everything that you and your child do together. As you recite nursery rhymes to your baby, read his favorite book, or talk about the crunchy red apple he is eating, you are stimulating his language development. If possible, let your child accompany you to the supermarket, post office, and dry cleaners, and talk to him about what he is seeing, doing, and thinking.

TALK, TALK, TALK

The experts agree that the more language your baby hears and the more responsive you are to his communications—even his earliest babbles—the more his inborn ability to acquire language will be enhanced. Research tells us that by talking to your baby, you actually can strengthen the pathways in his brain, which will enhance his learning ability throughout his life. In the next chapter, we will discuss talking techniques and how to put your *Thoughts* and *Actions* into words to enhance your child's *Language* and *Knowledge*.

4

The Five Methods
of Language Learning

Before a child can speak or use expressive language, she must understand words. In order to understand words, a child must know the meanings of those words—that is, what actions, objects, or thoughts those words represent. The natural way for your baby to learn the meanings of words is to listen to you talk in relation to the events going on around you. In this manner, she will learn to associate the words you say with the actions, objects, or thoughts you describe.

Most babies are surrounded by conversation from birth on. But it is also important that they be spoken to directly long before they can talk back. Just because a baby isn't talking yet, it doesn't mean she is not listening and learning the meanings of words and actions. In this chapter, we will discuss the best ways of talking to babies, as well as the five methods for helping your baby learn to talk.

TALKING TECHNIQUES

When talking to young children, people all over the world tend to use a high-pitched, singsong speaking style known as "parentese." When using this technique, adults also often change the words they use, their rate of speaking, and their loudness level. Researchers continue to debate if talking in parentese to children helps or hinders their language development. However, most people agree that the following talking techniques can help children learn to talk.

Talk About What Is Happening Around You

It will be easier for your child to understand and express words if you talk about the people, objects, and events around you. This will help your child relate your words to the things she is seeing, hearing, smelling, and tasting.

Experts believe that there are two talking techniques that children enjoy. One is called *self-talk*. In this technique, you talk out loud about what you are seeing, feeling, hearing, and touching. Self-talk can be used with any activity.

 TALKING TIME

Following is an example of an adult using self-talk:

Adult using self-talk: "I am looking for my blue hat. Here it is!"

As this parent talks, the baby learns that there are words to represent what the parent is doing.

The second talking technique is called *parallel talk*. In this technique, you talk out loud about what your baby is seeing, feeling, hearing, and touching. Parallel talk also can be used with any activity.

 TALKING TIME

Following is an example of an adult using parallel talk:

Adult using parallel talk: "You are splashing in the bathtub."

As this parent talks about what the baby is doing, the baby learns that words go with her actions as she relates what she is doing to the words her parent is saying.

Speak slowly and clearly to your child. If you speak at a slow, but comfortable pace and enunciate clearly, it will be easier for your child to learn the individual words. Emphasizing and repeating words may also help.

TALKING TIME

Following is an example of an adult using repetition:

Adult using repetition: "See the sock. It goes on your foot. *Foot.*"

It is important to emphasize and repeat words because children must hear a word many times before they can connect a meaning to it and eventually say it.

Use Short Phrases and Sentences

Researchers have found that if you talk to your child using short phrases and sentences, your child may grasp the rules of grammar more easily. However, don't abandon longer sentences altogether. Studies have also shown that toddlers whose parents sometimes use word phrases joined by words such as "because" and "which" tend to use complex sentences earlier than those whose parents do not.

 TALKING TIME

Following are examples of an adult using short and complex sentences:

Adult using a short sentence: "Your coat is blue."

Adult using a complex sentence: "You wear mittens because it is cold."

Use Expansion

When your child begins to say words, it is important to respond to her efforts to communicate in a positive way. By using the techniques of *expansion* and *expansion plus,* you give your child positive feedback. You let her know that you are listening, and that you understand and approve of her message. This will encourage her to keep trying and learning.

To use *expansion,* repeat what your child says and expand her utterance by adding one or two words. Do not change your child's meaning, but instead, make her remark slightly longer.

 TALKING TIME

Following is an example of an adult using expansion:

Child: "Hat."

Adult using expansion: "Yes, blue hat."

This adult did not change the child's message. However, by adding "yes" and "blue," the adult exposed the child to more words and let her know that the message was understood.

When you use *expansion plus*, you help your child clarify her message. In this technique, you repeat what your child says, then add appropriate grammar and an additional sentence or two. Again, by using this technique, you will let your child know that you understand and approve of her message.

 TALKING TIME

Following is an example of an adult using expansion plus:

Child: "My blue hat."

Adult using expansion plus: "Yes, it is your blue hat. I bought it for you at the mall."

To use expansion plus, follow your child's lead and talk about what she is interested in. You will provide your child with a good model of how words go together, and will help her learn how to expand her own utterances.

THE FIVE METHODS OF LANGUAGE LEARNING

Imagine that you and a friend are visiting a foreign country. The language is unfamiliar to you, and you are each staying at the home of a different family. In the house where you are staying, your hosts take an active part in helping you learn the language. They show you things, and name objects, people, and events. They compare and describe things by talking about colors, shapes, textures, and sizes. They explain how items are the same, how they are different, and how they are used. They talk about events in a logical order, and explain why things happen when they happen. They do all of this in your natural environment, as you go about your daily activities. As a result, you begin to understand words and concepts in the new language, and begin to use that language to communicate your own thoughts and feelings.

However, at the home where your friend is staying, the family members know that she can't speak the language, so they just don't talk to her. Your friend is simply surrounded by conversational speech. Sometimes, her hosts ask her questions, but she is not able to understand or respond. They may ask her to repeat their words and phrases, but she is having difficulty connecting meanings and actions to the words of the foreign language, and is unable to express herself.

Think of your baby as a traveler learning a new language. Your baby must understand the words in order to use them in a meaningful way. Instead of asking her a lot of questions or requiring her to repeat what you say, you should talk to her. Put your thoughts and actions into words, and tell her what you are seeing, doing, and thinking using the five language-learning methods. Use naming to teach your child word labels, or nouns. Use describing to teach your child about the qualities of objects and events, such as color and sound. Use comparing to teach your child about how objects, events, and people are the same or different. Use explaining to teach yoru child about time and logical order, as well as action words and things that go together. Use direction giving to teach your child about spatial concepts. These methods focus on improving a child's understanding of language. You can use them alone or simultaneously as you simply, but attentively, talk to your child in her natural environment.

Method One—Naming

Your child will recognize familiar objects long before she knows what they are called. The world of a one-year-old is filled with things with "unknown names" that are simply acquired by grunting and pointing. Your baby must learn the basic rule that everything has a specific name, or label.

Another type of name your child must learn is the category name. Categories are groups of words to which many things belong. Knowledge of categories helps your child make associations and link new information to words she already knows. This is important because our world is arranged by categories. For example, if you want to buy an apple, you don't go to the apple store, but rather, to a food store or fruit stand. You take a trip to the zoo to see animals, and to a toy store to buy toys. The categories into which your baby divides her world will continually change and grow in number as she continues to learn more and more.

*"This is a hat. **Hat**."*

How to Use Naming

To use naming to teach your child language, draw her attention to an object or event. At the same time, name the object or event. You can use a single word, such as "hat," or a short phrase, such as, "This is a hat." You can stress the label by saying it louder or repeating it: "This is a hat. Hat."

Method Two—Describing

When you talk about objects and events, describe their qualities. Their qualities can include color, shape, size, texture, and sound. When you describe objects and events in terms of their qualities, you will help your child learn to describe things this way. (For a discussion of how children learn about the qualities of color, size, shape, texture, and number, see "How Children Learn" on page 40.) As your child chooses how to describe things, she will also learn to express her own opinion. When you describe objects and events to your child, you will help her learn about numbers, too. This is because your descriptions will often include quantities, or "how much." Through the method of describing, your child will begin to understand and express words that tell about important details of her world.

"This is a big round ball."

How to Use Describing

To use describing to teach your child language, draw her attention to an object or event. At the same time, *describe* one or more qualities of the object or event. You can talk about its color (a green flower), or its shape and size (a big round ball). You can talk about its quantity (many apples, two dogs, a few raindrops), or its texture (soft hair, hard floor, slippery ice). Or, you can talk about the sound it makes (loud horn, noisy kids, squeaky door).

Method Three—Comparing

By helping your child recognize how items are the same and how they are different, you will help her learn about important details in her world. In order to make sense of the world, children must be able to see and understand that, for example, a cucumber is long while an orange is round, and a banana and a lemon are the same color. This is called *visual discrimination*. Children also must be able to hear the differences between "bag," "bat," and "bean" in order to understand what is being said to them. This is called *auditory discrimination*. We learn to recognize how things are the same or different by comparing them to each other.

"One dog is little and one dog is big."

How to Use Comparing

To use comparing to teach your child language, draw her attention to some objects, events, or people. At the same time, talk about how the objects, events, or people are the same and different, comparing their shapes, colors, sizes, textures, and/or sounds. You can also help your child learn about opposites (old shoe, new shoe; light box, heavy box; big dog, little dog) this way.

Also, talk about objects, events, or people that can be easily "compared" using words that end in "er" and "est." Point out to your child foods that are small, smaller, and smallest; trees that are tall, taller, and tallest; boxes that are big, bigger, and biggest; and hoses that are long, longer, and longest.

Method Four—Explaining

By explaining what you are seeing, doing, and/or thinking, you can teach your child a number of important concepts. Explaining what you are doing helps teach your child about the logical order of events. It can also help teach her about time. Time cannot be touched. It is an abstract concept that is not easily understood. A child's concept of time develops slowly as she lives in the here and now. Young children seem to become concerned with time only if they have to wait for something. Explaining what comes first or talking about what happened yesterday will help your child begin to understand what time is and how it passes.

Explaining how certain things go together can help your child take her first step in learning how to make choices and solve problems. For example, teaching your child that umbrellas and rain go together will help her learn how to remain dry on stormy days. Teaching her that soap goes with washing will help her learn how to make herself clean.

Explaining what you are doing can help your child learn about action words. Most children and adults build sentences using action words. We often talk about what objects or people can do, what they have already done, what they want to do, or what they may do next. In order for a statement to be meaningful, it usually needs an action word. When your young child is able to understand and express action words, she will be able to interact with her environment by giving directions, asking permission, or requesting information. Because most action words can be demonstrated, they can easily become meaningful to your child.

"We play baseball with a bat and ball."

How to Use Explaining

To use explaining to teach your child language as well as about time and the log-ical order of events, draw her attention to what you are doing. Talk about what you are doing first, and what you will do next. Use words and phrases such as "before dinner" and "after we go to the post office." Talk about things that hap-pened yesterday, things that are happening now, and things that may happen tomorrow.

To use explaining to teach your child language as well as about things that go together, draw her attention to some objects or events that belong together or have elements that do. At the same time, either say the words that go togeth-er (bat and ball, rain and raincoat), or explain how they go together ("We play baseball with a bat and ball," "You wear a raincoat when it rains").

To use explaining to teach your child language as well as action words, draw her attention to a person or object that is doing something (your child running, a boy playing on a swing). At the same time, talk about what is being done ("You are running," "The boy is swinging").

Method Five—Giving Directions

By giving your child directions, you can help her learn spatial-concept words, such as "on," "under," "around," and "over," as well as under-stand and follow simple directions. Everything, to a young child, is dependent on her own body position. The easiest way for a young child to learn about space is to move herself and objects in space. Children learn about their own body positions in relation to other people (on Mommy), and then in relation to other objects (on the table). Understanding spatial concepts will enable your child to follow many different kinds of direc-tions.

How to Give Directions

To use direction-giving to teach your child language, draw her attention to you and ask her to follow a simple direction. You can ask her to do something in rela-tion to herself ("Look in back of you") or in relation to an object ("Look under the table," "Put the toys in the box"). Try to use the following words often when you talk to her—"in," "on," "under," "over," "in front of," "behind," "next to," "top," "bottom," "around," and "inside."

"Look under the table."

Very quickly, using the five methods of language learning will become a habit, a special way of interacting with your young child. Talking can and should be a natural part of everything you and your child do together. Just like seeds in a garden, your baby's understanding of language needs to be nurtured in order to grow and bloom.

Now let's put the five methods into action and try using them on a trip to the supermarket, a place where most parents go at least once a week. With your child sitting in the cart facing you, it provides a great opportunity for talking!

How Children Learn

Most children learn new skills in all the areas of development in a specific order. Just as babies usually crawl before they walk, a child learning about color, shape, size, texture, and number will progress from the simplest to the more difficult tasks.

☐ **COLOR**

The same as with other words, children must first understand the color names before they can say them. The first color name that most children understand is that of their favorite color. Next, they learn to match colors. They then learn to point to colors upon request, and, finally, to say the names of colors.

"Point to the fruit that is yellow."

"This bottle is big, this one is bigger, and this one is the biggest."

❒ SIZE

Children usually begin to learn about size by nesting objects—that is, putting smaller objects into larger ones. Next, they learn to recognize and sort by size (all the big cups, all the little cups), and then to identify what size something is (big, little). Soon, they learn to use size words in conversation.

"Please get me two boxes of pasta."

☐ NUMBER

Children first learn the concept of "one." They demonstrate their knowledge by choosing or giving you one object. After "one," they learn "two," and after "two," they progress to the larger numbers. They learn first how to put a certain number of items in a group. Next, they learn to recognize how many items a group has. Finally, they learn to count items out loud.

❏ SHAPE

Research has shown that babies are born with the ability to recognize circles, squares, and triangles as three distinct shapes. Shape is one of the easiest ways to see how objects are different from each other. Experts believe that babies see the world as a puzzle. They must figure out where objects go—for example, shoes go on feet, and mittens go on hands. When a baby starts to do real puzzles, she uses what she learned about shape as an infant.

"Your boots go on your feet."

☐ **TEXTURE**

A number of experts believe that babies can distinguish some textures at birth. In experiments, babies who were given rough and smooth nipples to suck reacted differently to each. Babies become more sensitive to texture as they develop motor skills, and are able to move around, and feel and hold objects.

*"The sponge is bumpy, the towel is soft,
the soap is slippery."*

5

At the
Supermarket

*The five methods really work like nothing else has. As you know,
my son, Jake, has been a little slow to develop language skills.
The next time I was in the grocery store, I put your ideas into
practice, and by the time we left, he was saying "apples" and
"nanas." He loves to go to the grocery store now, and it's become
a special time of learning and interaction for both of us.*

        —Nancy, mother of eighteen-month-old Jake,
        Linwood, New Jersey

For adults, the word "supermarket" conjures up many images, including long lines, squeaky carts, and even high prices. But to young children, supermarkets are a delightful array of sounds, bright colors, and delicious smells. As you may know, it is very simple for a young child to get into mischief at the supermarket. Food is sometimes easy to grab, and that stainless steel strip along the front of the meat counter apparently is very tasty. For safety reasons, you really must keep your eyes on your child every second, so why not engage his attention with the sound of your voice. Talk to your child using the five methods of language learning—naming, describing, comparing, explaining, and giving directions. As you fill your cart with food, you can fill your child's mind with hundreds of words and phrases. Most likely, your child will be sitting in the shopping cart facing you. From this position, he can watch your every move. Think about it: Would you like to sit in a chair facing a familiar adult who has nothing to say? As you simply, but attentively talk to your child using the five methods, you can turn your trip to the supermarket into active, quality, sharing time spent with your young child.

In the following pages, the examples given for each of the five methods are only a few of the endless ways in which you can help your young child learn new words and concepts as you buy your week's groceries. Remember to follow your baby's lead, and be a good listener.

NAMING AT THE SUPERMARKET

As you put items in your cart, you have a monumental opportunity to improve your child's knowledge of words. By naming the items, you can help your child learn about word labels. You can also help your child learn about groups of words, or categories.

To use naming, engage your child's attention and name items as you pass them or put them in your cart:

❑ Napkins	❑ Fish
❑ Cake	❑ Grapes
❑ Juice	❑ Butter
❑ Can	❑ Bread

The supermarket is arranged by categories. As you turn the corner and begin to go down a new aisle, talk about the groups of items you see:

❑ Fruits	❑ Cereals
❑ Vegetables	❑ Poultry
❑ Cake mixes	❑ Paper products
❑ Soft drinks	❑ Cleaning products

DESCRIBING AT THE SUPERMARKET

In the produce section alone, you will find every color, texture, and shape imaginable to describe to your child. This is also a great place to teach your child about quantity by using words that describe how many or how much (more, less, few, several, one, one more).

To use describing, engage your child's attention and talk about the colors of the items you pass or put in your cart:

❑ *Green* peppers	❑ *Orange* carrots

❏ *Purple* grapes   ❏ *Brown* potatoes

❏ *White* mushrooms   ❏ *Blue* blueberries

Talk about the shapes of the items you see:

❏ *Flat* pea pods   ❏ *Long* spaghetti

❏ *Oval* eggs   ❏ *Square* and *triangular* cheeses

❏ *Round* rolls   ❏ *Rectangular* boxes

Talk about how items feel. Let your child touch some of the items, if possible.

❏ *Rough* pineapples   ❏ *Hard* carrots

❏ *Smooth* pears   ❏ *Soft* sponges

❏ *Bumpy* squash   ❏ *Sticky* candy

When you put produce in bags or items in your cart, talk about how many or how much you are taking:

❏ *One* box of raisins   ❏ *Several* onions

❏ *Many* potatoes   ❏ A *full* bag of apples

❏ A *few* cantaloupes   ❏ *One more* pear

As you pass through the aisles, talk about the sounds you hear:

❏ Door opening and   ❏ Employees talking
   closing

❏ Music playing on   ❏ Boxes falling
   the loudspeaker

❏ Wheels squeaking   ❏ Cash registers clicking

COMPARING AT THE SUPERMARKET

Most products come in different sizes. As you push your cart down the aisle, you are continually making choices. You may choose a large box of cereal, but a small bottle of salad dressing. Use words to compare the products you see and choose, and their locations. You will help your child learn about sizes and opposites.

To use comparing, engage your child's attention and compare the sizes of items you pass or put in your cart:

❏ This bag is *small*. This can is *big*. This box is *long*.

❏ This apple is *smaller* than the watermelon.

❏ This box is *big*. This box is *bigger*. This box is the *biggest*.

Talk about opposites using items you pass as examples:

❏ Ice cream is *cold*. Soup is *hot*.

❏ Cans are *heavy*. Napkins are *light*.

❏ Grapes are *small*. Watermelons are *large*.

To teach your child about opposites, you can also have him examine boxes: "Look at this cereal box. There is a rooster on the front of the box. There is a boy on the back of the box."

You can also have your child compare similar items to different items: "Look at all these apples. These apples are the same. These apples are different."

To teach opposites, you can also have your child do opposite things: "Look on the high shelf. Look on the low shelf."

EXPLAINING AT THE SUPERMARKET

As you push your cart down the aisle or place your groceries on the conveyor belt at the checkout counter, use words to explain what is happening. Your child will learn about the logical order of events and action words. In supermarkets, items that are used together are usually located near each other. Point them out and talk about how they are used to help your child learn about things that go together.

To use explaining, engage your child's attention and explain what you are seeing, doing, and thinking as you walk through the aisles.

To help your child learn about the logical order of events, use words that describe time:

❏ *First* we will shop. *Next* we will have lunch.

❏ You can eat this pretzel *now*. The rest are for *later*.

❏ *Soon* we will go home and see Tom.

To help your child learn about things that go together, talk about them as you put them in your cart or pass them in the aisles:

❏ Bread and butter   ❏ Spaghetti and sauce

❏ Toothbrush and toothpaste   ❏ Eggs and bacon

❏ Pancakes and syrup   ❏ Tortilla chips and salsa

To help your child learn about action words, talk about your actions as you shop:

- ❏ I am *pushing* the cart.
- ❏ I am *touching* the mangos.
- ❏ I am *opening* the freezer door.
- ❏ I am *lifting* the bag.
- ❏ We are *turning* the corner.
- ❏ I am *paying* the cashier.

GIVING DIRECTIONS AT THE SUPERMARKET

When you select the items you want to buy and place them in your cart, you have a natural opportunity to teach your child language using the method of direction-giving. You can also enlist your child's help at the checkout counter when you remove your selections from your cart and place them on the conveyor belt. Whenever possible, give your child simple directions using words that tell "where." You will not only foster your child's active participation, but will also teach him spatial concepts.

To use direction-giving, engage your child's attention and tell him to do something simple. Use words that describe positions in space:

- ❏ Put the apple *in* the bag.
- ❏ Watch me put the dog food *under* the cart.
- ❏ Put the cereal *next* to you.
- ❏ Put the bread *behind* you.
- ❏ Look *on the side* of the box.
- ❏ Look at the birdhouses *over* your head.

 TALKING TIME

Following is an example of an adult using all five methods of language learning on a trip to the supermarket:

Adult speaking to young child: "Let's buy some apples. Red apples, green apples. I want green ones. First, I tear off a bag. Next, I get the apples. They are round and shiny. One, two, three, four apples in the bag. I am closing the bag. Put the bag behind you."

Do you see how all five methods of language learning can be used in a natural manner? This parent helped his young child learn about names (apple, bag), colors (red, green), shapes (round), number concepts (one, two, three, four), spatial concepts (in, behind), and the logical order of events (first, next).

The next time you go to the supermarket with your young child, use the five methods of language learning. The knowledge you give your child will certainly be worth the few extra seconds it takes to count the apples you put in the bag. The supermarket is truly a smorgasbord of language-learning activities.

In the next chapter, we will take a look at how the five methods can be used at the playground.

6

At the Playground

I ran to the washer as it thumped and banged. It soon became obvious that my daughter and her grandmother had come back from the park with more than dirty shoes. However, the four little rocks in the bottom of my washer proved to be a valuable language lesson for my daughter. We talked about the different colors, shapes, and textures, and how the two biggest ones were the same. My daughter practiced making choices as she selected which one she liked the best each day. My daughter has continued to add to her "cowection" (her pronunciation) each time we go to the park. As she chooses, counts, describes, and categorizes her rocks, she is learning.

—Maria, mother of three-year-old Christine,
Harrisburg, Pennsylvania

Psychologists often view play as the way children explore the world and learn how to interact with it. Playing at the playground can be used as a medium for teaching language skills. In this chapter, we will take a look at how you can use the five methods of language learning while playing with your young child on playground equipment or even simply walking around the neighborhood or a park.

Your baby's first outings will likely include walks in her stroller or backpack to a nearby playground or park. As your baby receives the benefits of fresh air and sunshine, you can talk to her about what you are seeing and what others are doing. You can easily stop the stroller, lean down to her face, and direct her attention to an airplane flying overhead or a squirrel scurrying up a tree.

As your baby grows, she will become increasingly mobile and strong. Most toddlers love to explore. You can use the five methods of language learning not only to teach your toddler language, but to direct her attention to safer activities. The social interaction will also be invaluable for your child. She will not only learn from your words, but research has shown that children of all ages learn from watching each other.

NAMING AT THE PLAYGROUND

In an excited fashion, your young child may point, grunt, or just start running toward that special thing that catches her eye. Give your child names for what she sees and anticipates.

Research has shown that, at about two-and-a-half years of age, children begin to enjoy playing with others. Use naming to help your child develop social language skills. Show your child how to greet people and how to make introductions using word labels: "Nick, this is Anna. Hi, Anna." The playground is also a great place to teach your child about categories.

To use naming, engage your child's attention and name things you see or play with:

❏ Slide	❏ Sandbox
❏ Ladder	❏ Bush
❏ Jungle gym	❏ Mother
❏ Bar	❏ Seesaw

As you explore the playground, talk about groups of things you see:

❏ Toys to play on (sandbox, swing, seesaw)

❏ Animals (dogs, birds, squirrels)

❏ Plants (bushes, trees, flowers, grass)

DESCRIBING AT THE PLAYGROUND

As you play outside with your child, use words to describe nature's beauty. Your child will learn about colors, textures, sizes, shapes, and sounds.

At the playground, you usually see multiple items—for example, more than one animal, tree, or child. Count the items you see to help your child learn about quantity.

To use describing, engage your child's attention and talk about the colors that are all around you:

☐ *Green* grass   ☐ *Yellow* flowers

☐ *Blue* Sky   ☐ *Red* bird

☐ *White* clouds   ☐ *Brown* dirt

Talk about the shapes you see at the playground:

☐ *Round* merry-go-round   ☐ *Long* bars

☐ *Oval* chain links   ☐ *Short* steps

☐ *Square* swing seats   ☐ *Round* tunnel

Talk about how things feel at the playground:

☐ *Cold* bars   ☐ *Smooth* stones

☐ *Slippery* slide   ☐ *Rough* tree bark

☐ *Bumpy* chain   ☐ *Soft* sand

As your child plays on the equipment, use words that describe how many or how much:

☐ *Five* trips down the slide   ☐ *One more* push on the swing

☐ *Six* steps up the ladder   ☐ *Several* boys on the jungle gym

☐ A *few* children playing   ☐ *Two* trees

Use words to describe the sounds you hear:

☐ Horns beeping   ☐ Swings squeaking

☐ Birds chirping   ☐ Motors running

☐ Children laughing   ☐ Brakes squeaking

COMPARING AT THE PLAYGROUND

Look around the playground and discuss how the things your child sees and plays with are the same and how they are different. This will help your child learn about sizes and opposites.

To use comparing, engage your child's attention and compare the sizes of the things you see or play with:

❐ The sandbox is *short.* The jungle gym is *tall.* The swing set is *wide.*

❐ The bush is *smaller* than the tree.

❐ That boy is *big.* That boy is *bigger.* That boy is the *biggest.*

Talk about opposites using playground equipment as examples:

❐ This slide is *curvy.* That slide is *straight.*

❐ Dogs are *noisy.* Bugs are *quiet.*

❐ The sandbox is *nearby.* The swing is *far away.*

To teach your child about opposites, you can also compare her actions:

❐ You are swinging *forward.* Now you are swinging *backward.*

❐ You are *running.* Now you are *standing still.*

❐ You are walking *fast.* Now you are walking *slowly.*

EXPLAINING AT THE PLAYGROUND

By explaining what you are seeing, doing, and thinking at the playground, you can help your child learn how to take turns, use good judgment, make choices, and solve conflicts. You can even help her learn basic safety rules. In addition, you can teach your child about the logical order of events, action words, and things that go together.

To use explaining, engage your child's attention and explain what you are seeing, doing, and thinking as you walk around the playground and play on the equipment.

To help your child learn about the logical order of events, use words that describe time:

❐ *First,* you go up the slide. *Next,* you go down.

❐ He is *first.* You are *last.*

❐ You will swing *after* the girl.

To help your child learn about action words, talk about your actions as you play:

❐ I am *pushing* the swing.

❐ We do not *walk* in front of a swing that is moving.

❐ We *hold* on to the railing as we *go* up.

To help your child learn about action words, you can also talk about animals you see:

❐ Dogs *run.*   ❐ Dogs *jump.*

❐ Cats *climb.*   ❐ Bugs *crawl.*

❐ Squirrels *eat.*   ❐ Birds *fly.*

To help your child learn about things that go together, talk about things you see that are similar or that are used together:

❐ Bat and ball   ❐ Brother and sister

❐ Ladder and slide   ❐ Sandbox and bucket

❐ Dog and leash   ❐ Baby and stroller

GIVING DIRECTIONS AT THE PLAYGROUND

When you give your child directions at the playground, you will not only help her learn spatial concepts, but also safety rules for when she becomes more independent. In addition, you can direct her attention to sounds and their sources.

To use direction-giving, engage your child's attention and tell her to do something simple. Use words that describe positions in space:

❐ Look *over* your head.

❐ Go *down* the slide.

❐ Look *behind* the slide. See the children. They are laughing. Listen.

 TALKING TIME

Following is an example of an adult using all five methods of language learning during an outing to the playground:

Adult speaking to young child: "You are on the swing. You are in front. I am behind you. I can push you. Forward and backward, forward and backward. Higher and higher. One, two, three, four, five. One more push. Stop. That was fun. What should we do next?"

Do you see how you can use all five methods of language learning as you slowly and attentively talk to your child at the playground? This parent helped her young child learn about position in space (on, in front of, behind), opposites (forward, backward), comparatives (higher), number concepts (one, two, one more), and logical order of events (next).

As the months pass, you will surely notice your young child becoming much stronger and more independent. But, as you can see, playing at the playground can stretch her mind and heart as well as her muscles. By listening to you talk, she will not only learn the meanings of words and concepts, but also labels for feelings, basic rules of safety, and valuable life skills such as taking turns, making choices, solving problems, and using good judgment.

In the next chapter, we will discuss how to use the five methods while taking a ride in a car.

7

In the Car

===

*David, age twenty-eight months, was placed in his car seat by
his mother early one Saturday morning. His family members
were excited as they loaded the car and headed to Grandmother's
house. David's mom told me how excited and surprised she was
when she heard a little voice from the back seat say, "Where we
go?" No one had explained to David where the family was
going, who they would see, and why they were going. A great
opportunity for valuable language learning had been lost.*

Many people consider the time spent driving to be wasted time.
For young children and their parents, however, it can be a wonderful time for learning language and other skills. For children in school
or preschool, it can also be a great place for reinforcing the skills learned
in class. As you drive, you see numbers, letters, words, and symbols
everywhere. At first, you may feel foolish talking in the car because your
child is in the back seat and you are in the front, eyes forward, watching
the road as your steer. You need to remember, however, that your dialogue will pay off as you help develop your child's language skills and
awareness of the world.

The suggestions in this chapter are not intended for use on long trips.
Unless your child is lulled to sleep by your car's motor, keeping him con-
tent on such a trip will most likely require strategic planning that is
beyond the scope of this book. The following suggestions are, however,

for the many times you and your young child ride around town, going to and from the mall or daycare, or simply doing errands. Use a car seat that is safe and affords your child a good view. If more than one adult is present, take turns riding in the back seat. When a child is very young, it is easier to engage his attention and point things out when you sit next to him.

Since sitting in the front seat, driving, with the baby secured in a car seat in the back does not allow eye contact, open your dialogue by saying your baby's name or an attention-getting word such as "look" or "see." If you are on a highway and there is nothing interesting to see, recite nursery rhymes, count out loud, sing your child's favorite song, or talk about a trip to the park or zoo. You can even just say or sing your grocery list out loud: "We need some fruit—apples, bananas, and pears. Vegetables, too— onions, tomatoes, and celery. We need drinks—milk, apple juice, and tea." If your baby joins in, remember to be a good listener, and follow his lead.

NAMING IN THE CAR

The family car is not only a means of transportation to the supermarket, dry cleaner, and doctor's office, but also a way of providing your child with a cornucopia of sights and sounds to marvel over and discuss. In the country, you can point out and name all kinds of foliage and animals, while in the city, you will find hundreds of people, buildings, and vehicles to label and categorize. If you are generally pressed for time, just varying your route as you run your errands will turn up different sights and sounds to give a boost to your child's language development.

To use naming, engage your child's attention and name things that you pass on the road:

❒	Car	❒	Post office
❒	Sign	❒	Train
❒	House	❒	Bus stop
❒	School	❒	Man

Name the letters on billboards and signs that you pass. Name the numbers. Name the pictures.

Say the names of the streets that you pass. Say the complete names, including "Road," "Street," "Avenue," "Lane," "Drive," and so on.

Since the world is made up of categories of things, riding in the car is an excellent time to teach your child about groups of words. As you drive down the road, talk about groups of things you see:

❑ Vehicles (cars, buses, campers, trailers, motorcycles, vans, ambulances, fire trucks, police cars, mail trucks, delivery trucks)

❑ Traffic control devices (stop signs, traffic lights, bicycle crossing signs, yield signs)

❑ Parts of your car (steering wheel, seats, lights, radio, windshield wipers, heater, seatbelts, car seat)

Talk about smaller categories of things within larger categories. For example, after discussing the category of vehicles, talk about vehicles that help us, such as ambulances and fire trucks.

DESCRIBING IN THE CAR

By describing what you see, you can help your child learn about colors, shapes, and number concepts. You can also talk about the sounds you hear inside and outside of your vehicle.

To use describing, engage your child's attention and talk about things you pass on the road.

Talk about the colors of things you see:

❑	*Red* stop sign	❑	*White* house
❑	*Green* traffic light	❑	*Brown* telephone poles
❑	*Yellow* yield sign	❑	*Black* roofs

Talk about the shapes of things you see:

❑	*Round* tires	❑	*Triangular* pine trees
❑	*Oval* clouds	❑	*Diamond*-shaped signs
❑	*Rectangular* houses	❑	*Square* windows

As you drive down the road, count things that you see. Use words that describe how many or how much:

❑	*One* stoplight	❑	*A lot* of stores
❑	*Three* people crossing the street	❑	*One more* block to go
❑	*Several* people in a car	❑	*Many* birds

Talk about the sounds you hear inside and outside of your vehicle:

- ❐ Car motors running
- ❐ Turn signal clicking
- ❐ Radio music playing
- ❐ Car doors slamming
- ❐ Sirens roaring
- ❐ Car horns honking

COMPARING IN THE CAR

Compare the things surrounding you as you drive down the road or stop at a red light. Your child will learn about sizes and opposites.

To use comparing, engage your child's attention and compare the sizes of things that you pass:

- ❐ That car is *small.* That car is *big.*
- ❐ That sign is *small.* That sign is *smaller.* That sign is the *smallest.*
- ❐ The bus is *longer* than the taxi.

Talk about things you see that are the same as and different than each other:

- ❐ That car is the same color as our car.
- ❐ The truck is a different color than the bus.
- ❐ The arrow on the sign is curved. The arrow on the van is straight.

Talk about the weather:

- ❐ Yesterday it *rained.* Today it is *sunny.*
- ❐ It is *cold* in the winter. It is *hot* in the summer.
- ❐ It is *windy* in the winter. It is *not windy* in the summer.

EXPLAINING IN THE CAR

Before you even leave your driveway, use explaining to help your child learn about the logical order of events. Talk about why you are going, when you are going, what you will do when you reach where you are going, and whom you might see. Help your child learn about action words by talking about what you are doing now and what you will do when you get to your destination.

To use explaining, engage your child's attention and explain why you are in the car.

Talk about where you are going. To help your child learn about the logical order of events, use words that describe time:

❐ *First,* we will go to the post office. *Next,* we will go to the gas station.

❐ We are going to the supermarket *now.* We will play with Tom *later.*

❐ *Soon* we will be home again.

Talk about why you are going to where you are going:

❐ We are going to the post office because we need stamps.

❐ We are stopping at the gas station because the car needs gas.

❐ We are going to the supermarket because we need bread and milk.

Talk about what you will do when you reach your destination:

❐ We will buy stamps at the post office.

❐ We will put gas in the car at the gas station.

❐ We will buy bread and milk at the supermarket.

Talk about whom or what you might see:

❐ We will see a lot of post office boxes where the mail carriers put letters.

❐ We will see pumps that have gas to put in the car.

❐ We will see all different kinds of foods.

Talk about how long it will take to get there and when you will return home:

❐ It is a short trip. We will go home soon and have lunch.

❐ This may take a while, but we will play with Tom when we get home.

❐ We will go to four stores, then we will go home and make dinner.

Talk about what you are doing or will do to get to your destination:

❐ I am backing out of the driveway.

❐ I am turning right.

❐ I am turning left.

❐ I will drive straight.

❐ I will stop.

❐ I am parking the car so that we can go into the post office.

GIVING DIRECTIONS IN THE CAR

As you drive down the road, talk about people and things that you pass. Give your child simple directions using words that involve positions in space. This will help your child learn spatial concepts. If you are stopped in traffic or at a red light or stop sign, you may be able to safely turn your head in the direction you are talking about. If not, tell your baby to look out the window closest to you. Then, as you drive, you can narrate what you see.

To use direction-giving, engage your child's attention and tell him to do something simple:

❏ Look at the car in front of us. See the dog.

❏ Look at the car on the right side. It is blue.

❏ Look out the window. See the bird.

TALKING TIME

Following is an example of an adult using all five methods of language learning while riding in a car:

Adult speaking to young child: "Nick, we are going to the bakery. We will buy a cake for Tom's birthday. Look at the car beside us. See the big dog in the car. His head is out of the window. Look, here's a red stop sign on the corner. I will stop and look both ways. Look at the cake on the sign. This is the bakery."

Do you see how all five methods of language learning are used when you talk to your child about what you are thinking, seeing, and doing as you drive? This parent helped his young child learn about the logical order of events, spatial concepts (corner, on, beside), opposites (in, out), and colors (red).

During some trips, you may want to focus on just one idea or concept. For example, you can have your child point out all the circles he can find, look for things of one specific color, count all the animals, talk about all the sounds he hears, or look for arrows and talk about where they point. The possibilities are endless.

In the next chapter, we will take a look at how the five methods can be used at home as you and your child spend time together.

8

Around
the Home

==

We purchased our first home when my son was just two years old. Each room seemed to have hundreds of needed repairs. I remember my son following me around the house, holding his toolbox with the plastic tools, and asking, "What's that?" As I hammered, scraped, and painted, I answered his endless questions and narrated my actions. Consequently, as a three-year-old, he knew the names of most tools and could run his hand on the seam of the drywall and tell me if it was smooth or rough. I had found a way to be with my son, stimulate his language, and do my home repairs.

—Joe, father of two young boys,
Wildwood Crest, New Jersey

There is nothing more logical than to teach your child language skills in your own home. Your home is your child's natural environment. She is familiar with it and feels comfortable there.

This chapter highlights two activities that parents perform every day, in almost the same sequence each time—dressing the baby and bathing the baby. Your child is directly involved in these activities, and she has your undivided attention. As she is exposed to these same routines day after day and listens to you talk about them, she will be able to attach meanings to your words. This chapter also presents suggestions for other routine household activities to enjoy with your baby.

NAMING WHILE DRESSING

While dressing your child, you can help her learn language by using many different words that are a natural part of the dressing routine. You can talk about body parts, different kinds of clothes, parts of clothes items, and even where clothes are stored. This will help boost your child's knowledge of word labels and categories.

To use naming, engage your child's attention and name body parts as you dress her:

❐ Head	❐ Hands
❐ Nose	❐ Legs
❐ Ears	❐ Feet
❐ Arms	❐ Stomach

Name the clothes items you put on your child:

❐ Diaper	❐ Pants
❐ Underpants	❐ Socks
❐ Undershirt	❐ Shoes
❐ Blouse	❐ Sweater

Reinforce how to use pronouns (your nose, your clothes).
Match the body parts to the different clothing items:

❐ Pull your shirt over your head.	❐ Your legs go in your pants.
❐ Your socks go on your feet.	❐ Your hat goes on your head.
❐ Your belt goes around your waist.	❐ Put the mittens on your hands.

Name the parts of the clothes items:

❐ Sleeve	❐ Buttonhole
❐ Collar	❐ Cuff
❐ Zipper	❐ Shoelace
❐ Button	❐ Hood

Clothes are stored by category. As you take the different clothes items from where they are stored, discuss what kinds of clothes are kept where:

❐ Dresses in the closet	❐ Dirty clothes in the hamper
❐ Tee shirts in the bureau	❐ Coats in the coat closet
❐ Shoes under the bed	❐ Socks in the dresser

DESCRIBING WHILE DRESSING

By describing your child's clothes as you dress her, you will teach her about color, size, shape, and texture. Talk about clothes items that come in pairs to help her learn about quantity.

To use describing, engage your child's attention and talk about the colors of the different clothes items. Talk about the shade of the colors and the patterns:

- ❐ *Light blue* shorts
- ❐ *Plaid* shirt
- ❐ *Dark green* overalls
- ❐ *Striped* pants
- ❐ *Bright red* sneakers
- ❐ *Dotted* socks

Talk about how the clothes items feel:

- ❐ *Soft* sweater
- ❐ *Stretchy* elastic
- ❐ *Hard* jeans
- ❐ *Smooth* nylon
- ❐ *Bumpy* corduroy
- ❐ *Fuzzy* hat

Count how many pieces of each clothes item you put on her:

- ❐ *Two* shoes
- ❐ *One* sweater
- ❐ *Two* mittens
- ❐ *One* coat
- ❐ *One* shirt
- ❐ *One* pair of pants

Count the total number of clothes items you put on your child.

Talk about any numbers or letters on clothes items. Talk about the number inside each clothes item that indicates the size.

Talk about any pictures on clothes items and the shapes that compose them.

Talk about the different parts of the clothes items:

- ❐ *Bumpy* zipper
- ❐ *Loose* sweater
- ❐ *Square* buttons
- ❐ *Shiny* boots
- ❐ *Round* snaps
- ❐ *Blue* hat

Sing "One, Two, Buckle My Shoe."

COMPARING WHILE DRESSING

As you dress your child, use comparing to help her learn about sizes and opposites. Talk about the sizes of her clothes, as well as the sizes of other family members' clothes. Help her learn about opposites as you compare clothes or other items in her room.

To use comparing, engage your child's attention and compare the sizes of different clothes items:

❒ Pants are *longer* than shorts.

❒ This shirt is *large*. This shirt is *larger*. This shirt is the *largest*.

❒ This dress is too *loose*.

Talk about opposites using clothes items:

❒ These shoes are *old*. These shoes are *new*.

❒ Look at these *dirty* socks. Look at these *clean* socks.

❒ The shirt *front* has buttons. The shirt *back* does not.

To teach your child about opposites, you can also discuss how her clothes are similar to and different from your clothes.

To teach opposites, you can additionally have your child use her furniture:

❒ The top drawer is *open*. The bottom drawer is *closed*.

❒ *Open* the closet door. Now *close* the closet door.

❒ This drawer is *full*, but that drawer is *empty*.

EXPLAINING WHILE DRESSING

Use explaining while dressing your child to help her learn about the logical order of events, action words, and things that go together. Dressing is a predictable series of actions that happens at least twice a day. Talk about what you are doing now and what will happen after you have finished dressing her.

To use explaining, engage your child's attention and talk about the process of getting dressed.

To help your child learn about the logical order of events, use words that describe time:

❒ *First,* we put on your socks. *Next,* we put on your shoes.

❒ We will put your coat on *now. Then,* we will put on your mittens.

❒ *After* we get dressed, we will eat breakfast.

Talk about clothes items that go together:

- ☐ Hat and coat
- ☐ Shoes and socks
- ☐ Shirt and pants
- ☐ Underwear and undershirt
- ☐ Jumper and blouse
- ☐ Raincoat and rain hat

To help your child learn about action words, talk about your actions while getting her dressed:

- ☐ We *pull* up your pants.
- ☐ You *raise* your arms.
- ☐ We *button* the buttons.
- ☐ We *zip* the zipper.
- ☐ We *tie* your shoes.
- ☐ We *put* the hat on your head.

GIVING DIRECTIONS WHILE DRESSING

Give your child simple directions while getting her dressed to ensure her active participation and to teach her spatial concepts.

To use direction-giving, engage your child's attention and tell her to do something simple. Use words that describe positions in space:

- ☐ Watch me put your shoe *on* your foot.
- ☐ Put your arm *in* the sleeve.
- ☐ Help me pull the sweater *over* your head.

 TALKING TIME

Following is an example of an adult using all five methods of language learning while dressing her young child:

Adult speaking to young child: "Let's put your socks and shoes on. Two white socks. Give me your foot. First your socks. One sock on, one sock off. Two socks on. Let's put your shoes on next. I am tying your shoes so that they won't fall off."

This parent helped her young child learn about word labels (shoes, socks, foot), colors (white), number concepts (one, two), logical order of events (first, next), action words (tying, putting, fall), and opposites (on, off).

In the next part of this chapter, we will take a look at how the five methods can be used during bath time. The bathtub is a great place to enhance language. Most children love to take baths. Your child has your undivided attention, making it a great time to talk, play, and enjoy each other.

NAMING DURING BATH TIME

While bathing your child, name her body parts and things around her to help her learn word labels. Talk about groups of words that go together to help her learn about categories.

To use naming, engage your child's attention and name the bath items you use:

❑ Rubber duck	❑ Drain
❑ Soap	❑ Tub
❑ Towel	❑ Water
❑ Washcloth	❑ Shampoo

Name your child's body parts as you wash or dry them.
Talk about groups of things connected with the bath:

❑ Bath toys (rubber duck, busy box, sailboat)

❑ Body parts (arm, foot, nose)

❑ Parts of the bathtub (drain, faucet, bathmat)

DESCRIBING DURING BATH TIME

While bathing your baby, describe the bath items you use to help your child learn about colors and textures. Count her body parts to help her learn number concepts.

To use describing, engage your child's attention and talk about the colors of bath items:

❑ *Green* soap	❑ *Blue* shower curtain
❑ *Yellow* rubber duck	❑ *Red* pail
❑ *White* towel	❑ *Yellow* shampoo

Talk about how the items feel:

- ❐ *Slippery* soap
- ❐ *Soft* bath towel
- ❐ *Rough* washcloth
- ❐ *Hard* tub
- ❐ *Smooth* shampoo bottle
- ❐ *Cold* faucet

Bath time is a great time to learn number concepts. When you wash your child, count her body parts:

- ❐ *One* arm, *two* arms
- ❐ *One* toe, *two* toes, *three* toes . . . *ten* toes
- ❐ *One* nose
- ❐ *One* finger, *two* fingers, *three* fingers . . . *ten* fingers
- ❐ *One* leg, *two* legs
- ❐ *One* ear, *two* ears

COMPARING DURING BATH TIME

Use comparing while bathing your child to help her learn about sizes and opposites. Talk about body parts as well as things around you.

To use comparing, engage your child's attention and compare the sizes of different bath items:

- ❐ The towel is *bigger* than the washcloth.
- ❐ The soap is *smaller* than the shampoo bottle.
- ❐ This boat is *big*. This boat is *bigger*. This boat is the *biggest*.

Talk about opposites:

- ❐ You are *dirty*. Soap will make you *clean*.
- ❐ The tub is *empty*. Let's turn on the water. Soon it will be *full* of water.
- ❐ You are *out* of the tub. Get *in* the tub.

EXPLAINING DURING BATH TIME

Taking a bath, the same as getting dressed, involves a predictable series of events. Talk about what you are doing now as well as what you will do later. Explain what you are doing and seeing to help your child learn about action words and things that go together.

To use explaining, engage your child's attention and explain what you are doing as you bathe her.

To help your child learn about the logical order of events, use words that describe time:

❏ *First,* you will take a bath. *Next,* you will put on your clothes.

❏ *First,* we wet your hair. *Next,* we put on the shampoo.

❏ *Before* you take a bath, you are dirty. *After* you take a bath, you are clean.

If you give your child a bath in the morning, talk about what you will do later that day. If you give your child a bath at night, talk about what you did that day and what you plan to do the next.

Talk about things that go together or are used together during or after a bath:

❏ Soap and washcloth   ❏ Shampoo and hair

❏ Water and sailboat   ❏ Toothbrush and toothpaste

❏ Brush and comb   ❏ Baby lotion and baby powder

To help your child learn about action words, talk about the things you are doing during the bath:

❏ We are *washing* your tummy.   ❏ You are *wiggling* your toes.

❏ We are *rinsing* your hair.   ❏ We are *drying* your face.

❏ You are *kicking* your legs.   ❏ I am *splashing* you with water.

GIVING DIRECTIONS DURING BATH TIME

As you give your child simple directions during her bath, you will help her learn spatial concepts.

To use direction-giving, engage your child's attention and tell her to do something simple. Use words that describe positions in space:

❏ Tilt your head *back.*   ❏ Look *up* at the showerhead.

❏ Put the duck *under* the water. ❏ Sit *down.*

❏ Put your hands *in* the water.   ❏ Put the boat *on* the water.

The five methods of language learning can all be used in a natural manner as you talk to your child while bathing her. This parent helped her young child learn about word labels (tub, water, soap, arm, legs, shirt), colors (blue), opposites (empty, full, clean, dirty, in, out), and spatial concepts (in, under).

TALKING TIME

Following is an example of an adult using all five methods of language learning during bath time:

Adult speaking to young child: "The tub is empty. Let's turn on the water. We are taking off your blue shirt. The tub is full of warm water. Get in the tub. Find the soap. It is under the water. Let's wash your arms. One arm, two arms. Your arms are clean. Your legs are dirty. Let's wash them next."

OTHER ACTIVITIES AROUND THE HOME

Daily life affords parents hundreds of opportunities to enhance their child's language skills. You don't have to buy expensive toys or devote time to flashing picture cards. Instead, the activities in your daily routine can be your tools. You can use the five methods of language learning (naming, describing, comparing, explaining, and giving directions) as you go about any activity in your home. Talk to your child about what you are doing, seeing, feeling, and touching as you cook dinner, vacuum the carpet, set the table, or sort and fold the laundry. Describe your actions as you make the bed, bake cookies, or simply pour your child a drink. Talk about the shiny tin foil and let her see her reflection as you pack sandwiches for lunch. No matter what the activity, just talk about it to enhance your child's language and learning. To a young child, the whole world is new. Even the most routine activities can be exciting and a learning experience for her. Just remember to follow your child's lead and to be a good listener.

> *Everyday life provides ideal tools for mental stimulation. There are teachable moments everywhere.*
> —Gloria Rodriguez, PhD, founder and president of
> Avance, a family-support program in San Antonio, Texas

In this chapter, you learned some of the ways in which you can use the five methods of language learning in your home. You saw that any activity in which you and your baby participate can be a language-learning experience. Remember, talking can and should be a part of everything you and your baby do together.

In the next chapter, we will take a look at the stages of language development. You will also find lists of brain-boosting tips and toys appropriate for the different stages of development.

9

The Stages of Language Development

"Is he talking as he should?"
"When will he talk?"
"Will you just check to make sure he's doing okay?"

Parents are always looking for reassurance that their children are growing and developing to their full potential. It is important to know what you can expect from your baby at each stage of development. In this chapter, we will discuss what most babies do at certain ages. The guidelines presented are simply that—guidelines. Some children develop certain skills earlier than most, and some develop them later. What is important is that a baby show continued progression from one stage to the next. Of course, if you have any concerns about your child's development in any area, you should seek professional help as soon as possible.

BEFORE THE FIRST WORD

Although most babies do not say their first word until they are roughly twelve months of age, they spend their first year preparing for that show-stopping moment by learning the language and practicing how to use their tongues, lips, and breathing. The first year of language development is divided into three distinct stages—birth to six months, six to nine months, and nine to twelve months. At the end of this section, you will find a list of brain-boosting tips and toys to use with your baby during these stages of language development.

Birth to Six Months

From the moment of birth, babies with normal hearing have the ability to listen to the sounds around them. By day three, they can recognize their mother's voice. By day nine, their eyes can track sounds. And by day fourteen, they can tell when their mother is near. Scientists believe that babies are able to do this because they recognize their mother's voice and scent from all the cuddling.

New parents tend to talk to their newborn almost nose-to-nose. Because of this, newborns can see their parents' faces—and playful expressions—clearly. By one month of age, babies already try to talk back. They open and close their mouths, and poke out their tongues to imitate their parents' speech. Since their vocal cords, mouths, and tongues are not very strong, they use crying to communicate. When they cry, they are practicing using their vocal cords, and they change the pitch and volume of their cry to communicate if they are hungry, tired, or simply discontented. Most parents learn quickly to recognize and appropriately respond to their babies' special cries.

At around three months of age, babies are better able to control the vocal muscles of their mouth and the larynx in their throat. They can even make sounds, such as "goo," in the back of their throat. They recognize inflection and tone of voice, and seem to understand when Grandma is asking them a question, Mom is telling them about something, and Dad is happy.

At five months old, babies can make a lot of sounds. They love to squeal, yell, and, occasionally, laugh out loud. Sometimes, they sound as if they are growling.

Babies' experiments with sounds, or "vocal play," contain many vowels, such as "ee" and "aa." They say these vowel sounds high and low, loud and soft. Their throat muscles are not yet fully developed, and these sounds are the easiest ones for them to make. They like to make the sounds after hearing people talk to them. Some babies can hold the sounds for a long time and say them very loud. At six months of age, they can also make sounds with the mouth partially closed (consonant sounds). Sometimes, they use just their lips to say "b," "m," or "p," or try to use their tongue to say "d," "l," or "t." Occasionally, it sounds as if they are trying to say syllables, since they sometimes put vowel and consonant sounds together ("ba," "ta," "bu"). Babies seem to enjoy talking and playing with sounds, especially before falling to sleep.

TALKING TIME

Following is an example of a four-month-old baby "talking":

Adult: "Let's put your hat on your head. It's cold outside today."
Four-month-old baby: Watches adult's face and lips. "Eee-eee."
Adult: "Eee-eee."

Six to Nine Months

Babies six to nine months of age are just starting to become true communicators. They love to laugh out loud and make raspberries. They are beginning to make early true language sounds. They seem to enjoy putting vowel and consonant sounds together and repeating them over and over again. Favorites are "baba," "dada," and "gaga." Technically, this is called "babbling." They do not have any idea what the sounds mean; they just seem to like making them. Sometimes, they closely watch the mouth of someone speaking to them and try to imitate the person's sounds and inflections. This way, they learn that new sounds can be made by changing the shape of the mouth. (For a discussion of babbling, see page 76.)

 TALKING TIME

Following is an example of a nine-month-old baby "talking":

Adult: "Let's put your jacket on. It's a little cool today."
Nine-month-old child: Excitedly moves legs and hands. "Wawawa."
Adult: "Yes, I am happy, too. Let's play outside."

Nine to Twelve Months

At nine months of age, babies can imitate many sounds, and can put vowels and consonants together to make real-sounding words. They can even make more than one sound in one breath, and use real tone and inflection. They recognize where words begin and end in their mother's stream of conversation. And even though they can't say any words yet, they now use sounds and gestures to talk to everyone. For example, a baby may say "mmmm" and put his hands up when he wants to be held. He may point

The Universal Language of Babbling

Researchers have concluded that all infants make the identical babbling sounds—"ba," "da," "ka," "ma," and "pa." It does not matter with which language the infant is surrounded. Remarkably, even deaf babies who cannot hear any language utter these sounds until six months of age. Researchers believe that a child's brain is actually programmed for babbling during the first six months of life. After that, babies begin to concentrate on the language that the people around them are speaking.

to his blanket and say "ahaha" when he is tired. When he sees a dog and wants to get down and touch it, he may move his arms and legs in an excited fashion. For a nine-month-old, these gestures and sounds are the way to communicate.

As babies approach their first birthday, they are able to understand more new words every day. A good method parents can use to check their baby's vocabulary is to say, "Show me," or to ask, "Where is —?" Babies at this age may point to or get the object that is being requested. At this age, memory seems to develop just as quickly as understanding. Many children are able to anticipate, for example, when their mother will tickle them or their father will say "Pop!" when singing "Pop Goes the Weasel."

Babies approaching their first birthday like to listen to their parents talk to each other and to them. They still babble a lot, but now they can also put different sounds together to make words such as "babana," "tada," and "pada." They often sound as if they are speaking a foreign language. Experts call it "jargon." Sometimes, a baby may raise his voice at the end as if he is asking a question. At times, a real-sounding word may be imbedded in the steady stream of jargon.

 TALKING TIME

Following is an example of an eleven-month-old baby "talking":

Adult: "Let's put on your bathing suit. We are going swimming."
Eleven-month-old baby: "Banama kada aah?"
Adult: "Yes, we are going in the pool."

Brain-Boosting Tips and Toys for Birth to Twelve Months

Use the following tips and toys to boost the language development of a child up to twelve months old:

❑ *Pay attention to your baby's special cries and gestures.* Find out what your baby's sounds and actions mean. Give him words for his feelings and actions. For example, if your baby seems to say "ahaahah" when he is tired, respond with, "You are tired. Go to sleep."

❑ *Play with sounds.* Respond to your baby's verbalizations, mouth movements, and hand gestures with imitation. When your baby smiles and coos, smile and coo back. When he babbles ("baba"), repeat what he says. At times, add another babbling sound ("babaga"). You can also vary his sounds by stretching them out, or saying them louder or quieter. Give him a chance to respond to your verbalizations before you begin again. When your baby is quiet, make one of his favorite sounds. See if he imitates you.

❑ *Address your baby by name.* Say his name when you talk to him, and talk about his belongings using the possessive (Tom's crib, Tom's dog). Use just one form of his name. Some experts believe that using more than one form (Tom, Tommy, Thomas) may be too confusing at this age.

❑ *Improve your baby's visual skills.* Help your baby learn to focus and to attend to what he is seeing. Position yourself at his eye level, about 8 to 12 inches from his face, and talk in a high-pitched voice or make faces as long as he is interested. You could also use a stuffed animal made in a "face front" style to do this. Children learn about facial expressions and how to make sounds by focusing on and attending to others. Research suggests that babies enjoy faces.

❑ *Help your baby develop memory skills.* Play the same games with your baby and sing the same songs. He will soon learn to anticipate your words and gestures. At around six months of age, he may acquire a favorite book. Although reading the same book four times in one morning (at your baby's request) may be tiring for you, the repetition will reinforce his learning. Reading the same words over and over will help him learn to make connections between the words he hears and the pictures he sees.

❑ *Help your baby learn thinking skills.* Help him learn to understand the following concepts so that he can learn to communicate with others:

- Object permanence—the concept that an object continues to exist even though you can no longer see it. Until your baby grasps this concept, he will not be able to give names to objects. This is because objects appear and disappear in his world. Comprehending the concept of object permanence will allow him to understand that a label is a name for an object whether it is seen or not.

    To develop the concept of object permanence, play peek-a-boo. At first, you may want to use something you can see through so that your face is never completely hidden from your baby when you hide behind the object. This will help your baby learn that you continue to exist. You also might wind up a musical toy, hide it under a cloth or pillow while the music is playing, and help your baby find it.

    While bathing your baby, place a floating toy in the water, cover it with a washcloth, and ask, "Where is the toy?" Then, lift the washcloth and say, "Here it is!" Repeat this a few more times, then encourage your baby to lift the cloth.

- Cause and effect—the concept that every action has a result or consequence. Your baby needs to know that if he does something, it can cause other things to happen. He must learn this to understand why people communicate. If you make a sound or say words, you get a desired result. For example, if one person smiles, another person will smile back.

    To develop the concept of cause and effect, help your baby shake plastic keys, rattles, or squeak toys. Encourage him to play with pop-up toys or busy boxes. In the bathtub, let him squeeze a sponge and watch water pour out. Your baby will learn that, by moving his hand, he can make things happen.

- Means to an end—the concept that you plan a course of action to accomplish a goal. This concept is used when you plan a language message to send to another person.

    To develop the concept of means to an end, use pull toys or push toys that require some planning to be made to move. Show your child how to use the toy, then let him play with it. For example, use a shovel to fill a pail with sand. Dump the sand, and let your child fill the pail.

❐ *Encourage your baby to imitate.* Attach an unbreakable mirror that has an accurate reflection to the side of your baby's crib. Look in the mirror with your baby, and talk about body parts. "I see your nose. I see my nose." Make mouth movements, such as sticking out your tongue and puffing up your cheeks, and encourage your child to imitate them. Make sounds for him to imitate. Imitate his sounds. Clinical research has suggested that babies make more sounds while they are looking in a mirror.

❏ *Encourage your baby to use gestures to communicate.* Raise his arms above his head and say, "So big!" Point to objects when you talk about them. Give him words for his gestures. For example, name what he points to. If he points to a dog, say, "There's a dog." Talk about what he signals with his body movements. If he shivers, say, "Br-r-r, it's cold."

❏ *Teach your baby to follow simple directions.* Hand him toys and ask him to hand them back to you.

❏ *Teach your baby about object qualities.* Play with nesting cups. Show your baby how some are big while others are small. Use them in the bathtub to demonstrate "full of water" and "empty." Use a ball to help your baby understand roundness. Let him feel the round shape. Roll the ball to him and say, "It is round. It rolls." Rub your baby's hand over the corners of a block and talk about the "square block." Use toys with different textures to teach him words that describe how things feel (smooth, soft, rough, bumpy, scratchy, hard). You can also put different kinds of balls (plastic, yarn, tennis) in a box, and let him feel them while you talk about their textures. Or, let him touch or handle a number of safe natural or household objects (soft sponge, hard rocks, rough carpet, hard table, bumpy chain).

For additional activities to help your child learn language and other skills, see Chapters 5 through 8.

ONE AND TWO WORDS

A child's second year of life is marked by learning to speak in one-word and then two-word "sentences." The year is divided into two distinct stages— twelve to eighteen months, and eighteen to twenty-four months. Again, at the end of this section, you will find a list of brain-boosting tips and toys to use with your child during these stages of language development.

Twelve to Eighteen Months

At about twelve months of age, most children say their first word. A child's first word is usually the name of something or someone that he has heard often. Repetition is the key, since the child must match what he sees with the word label he hears. In general, children's first words are very similar and fall into the following categories—names of people or objects that are important to the child (pop, dada, bottle), action words (up, eat), adjectives (more), and social words (bye-bye, hi).

The first word is followed by more and more new words. Sometimes, the first or last consonant or syllable will give the child trouble. However, parents tend to understand what their children are saying anyway, since most children continue to use gestures to help complete their thoughts. For example, while a child may say "da" instead of "dog," he will also point to the dog, thus making his meaning clear.

By sixteen months of age, most children can say about 25 words. However, they are able to understand about 170 words, including a number of action verbs (jump, open), tricky change-of-state verbs (put, give), adjectives (clean, soft, yucky), and adverbs (where). They can follow simple directions, and begin to use words to express their needs. For example, a sixteen-month-old will say "up" when he wants to be picked up, and "more" when he wants more food.

At seventeen months of age, children enter what experts call the "naming explosion." They finally realize that everything they see and do has a name. They love to imitate syllables and words said by other people, and to point to things to hear the label verbalized.

 TALKING TIME

Following is an example of a fourteen-month-old child talking:

Adult: "Let's put on your hat. We are going to the park to see the colorful leaves."

Fourteen-month-old child: "Hat."

Adult: "Blue hat."

Eighteen to Twenty-Four Months

At eighteen months of age, children can usually say about 50 words, and continue to understand many more words than they can say. In addition, they now are able to put two words together, saying things such as "more milk" and "up now," although they omit verb endings and unimportant words. For most children of this age, the vocabulary seems to explode, as they say a new word almost every day.

By twenty-four months of age, most children can say about 200 words. They often speak in two-word, and sometimes even three-word, sentences. They express that something is "mine," especially when playing with other children, and love to ask, "What's that?" Children of this age cannot yet say all the sounds of the language correctly, although their skills, in general, are greatly improved over what they were six months earlier. For example, they may say "tottie" for "cookie," or "nake" for "snake." Despite this, more than one-half of what a twenty-four-month-old says can be understood by others, compared to about one-quarter for an eighteen-month-old.

 TALKING TIME

Following is an example of a twenty-four-month-old child talking:

Adult: "Let's put on your hat. It's cold outside today."

Twenty-four-month-old child: "My hat."

Adult: "Yes, it's your blue hat."

Brain-Boosting Tips and Toys for Twelve to Twenty-Four Months

Use the following tips and toys to boost the language development of a child between twelve and twenty-four months old:

☐ *Give your child choices.* For example, if your child is pointing at the cupboard and whining, he may be having difficulty thinking of the word for what he wants. If you ask him, "Do you want a cookie or a cracker?" he will probably feel less frustrated as he responds to the choices. This will also help him learn to express his opinions and preferences.

☐ *Teach your child vocabulary words, action words, and concepts by encouraging him to help you around the house.* Give him push toys and toys similar to the tools you use around the house, and let him imitate you as you sweep, vacuum, or water the flowers. As you do your chores, talk about what you do first, next, and last: "First, we fill the bucket with water. Next, we dip the mop in the water." "Before we water the flowers, they are dry. Now, they are wet."

❑ *Help your child use words to describe and explain how he feels.* Encourage him to tell you what he feels and why. For example, say to him, "I know you are sad because we can't go to the park today."

❑ *Help your child practice word labels.* For example, when you read to your child, have him point to items, such as a cow or a fork, as you name them. For example, tell him to point to a cow. As a variation, have him point to categories, such as "animals" or "things we eat with."

❑ *Help your child expand his words and gestures into full ideas.* For example, if he points to a rabbit and says, "What's that?" tell him, "That's a rabbit. He is white and black. Look, he hops. Let's hop like a rabbit." Using this method, you will not only answer his question, but also will develop a whole idea about the rabbit.

For additional activities to help your child learn language and other skills, see Chapters 5 through 8.

A TRUE COMMUNICATOR

Children in their third year of life finally become "true communicators." The "true communicator" stage is considered to extend from the second birthday to the third. Once more, this section also offers a list of brain-boosting tips and toys to use with your child during this stage of language development.

Two to Three Years

By two and a half years of age, most children can understand about 800 words, and usually use 4 or 5 words at a time to express their feelings, wants, and needs. They understand instructions such as, "Put the toy in the box," "Put the hat on your head," and "Put the shoes under your bed."

Two-and-a-half-year-old children love to ask questions. Favorites are "Where is —?" "Who is —?" and "What is —?" They also like to answer questions such as "Where are you going?" or "What is this mess?" "They can follow directions such as "Get the bat and bring it to me," and "Tell daddy to get your sweater." They love to listen to books, and can even remember parts that have been read before.

By three years of age, most children's speech is much more sophisticated, since they now use sentences composed of a subject, verb, and object. They no longer speak in sentence fragments such as, "More milk," but instead use complete sentences such as, "I want some milk." They now refer to themselves as "I" or "me." They don't yet understand all the rules of grammar, however, so they do still make mistakes. For example, if we have two toys, why don't we have two feets? If we walked to the park, why didn't we runned home?

Brain-Boosting Tips and Toys for Two to Three Years

Use the following tips and toys to boost the language development of a child from two to three years old:

❐ *Help your child to be a good listener.* If you give him directions or have a conversation, eliminate distractions. Get his attention, perhaps by saying his name, before you start to talk; wait until he is looking at you before you begin to talk. Make eye contact. When reading a book to him, pause and ask simple questions such as, "Where did the boy go?" or "When will they eat the bread?"

❐ *Develop your child's knowledge and expression of basic concepts.* The best ways in which children learn about color, number, size, space, and position are playing, moving their bodies, and listening and talking to you. Some activities to try include:

- To teach your child about colors, have him name and/or match colors using Lego blocks. For example, tell him, "Find another one that looks like this one," or "Give me a blue block." Or, ask him, "What color is this?"

- To teach your child about numbers, first have him hand you one item. When he understands the concept of "one," progress to having him hand you larger numbers of items. Have him count body parts, stuffed animals, or cars on the road. Count and have him fill in the missing numbers: "One, two, —."

- To teach your child about size, draw short and long lines, or big and small circles with crayons on paper. Fashion big and small balls out of Play-Doh. Talk about things in terms of their sizes: "Elephants have long trunks. Rabbits have short legs." "Pigs have thin tails. Alligators have thick tails." Ask your child to identify items using size words: "Find the long string." "Where are your short pants?"

- To teach your child about space and position, give him directions to do things such as step *in* and *out* of a large box, walk *around* the box, stand *behind* or *in back* of the box, and get *under* the box. Blow bubbles and talk about how they land *behind* your head, *in front* of your head, *near* you, *far* from you, in the *corner* of the yard, and in the *center* of the yard. Discuss the *high* bubbles and the *low* bubbles.

❑ *Develop your child's memory.* Teach your child a nursery rhyme, short poem, or song. Repeat it a number of times, then leave off the final word and encourage your child to say it. Gradually leave off more words, and finally, whole lines. Soon, your child should be able to recite the whole verse. This is also a great way for your child to practice language and sounds.

❑ *Reinforce new concepts and words that your child learns.* When your child learns a new concept or word from a story, reinforce it in his natural environment. For example, after reading "The Little Red Hen" to your child, point out the bakery and the baker to him the next time he does errands with you. Show him the different kinds of bread at the bakery. Compare their shapes and sizes. Talk about how the baker made the bread.

❑ *Model correct responses for your child.* If your child says a word incorrectly, don't correct his speech by asking him to "say it again." Instead, model the correct response, emphasizing the word or sound with which he had difficulty. For example, if your child says, "Me do to pool," try saying, "*I g-go* to the pool." Emphasize "I" by saying it louder, and emphasize the "g" sound in "go" by stretching it. If you wish, point to your lips, tongue, or throat for additional emphasis. In addition, focus on what your child is saying correctly. Think of all he has learned in such a short amount of time. If your child senses that he is not talking correctly, he may become frustrated and stop talking.

If you are simply unable to understand what your child is saying, try smiling and understanding just one word. Use that word to ask your child a question. You could also ask your child to show you what he is talking about. If your child becomes frustrated, comfort him with pats or hugs, and say, "It's okay. I'm trying. Let me hear it again." (For methods to help your child learn better pronunciation, see "Ways to Stimulate Speech Sounds" on page 85.

❑ *Answer your child's questions, and ask him answerable questions.* Your child is now asking you questions to learn about his world. Answering those questions will not only give him knowledge, but will encourage him to

Ways to Stimulate Speech Sounds

To help your child's ability to say the various speech sounds, try the following activities. When saying a problematic speech sound, emphasize it by saying it louder and longer.

/b/ Wave bye-bye. Hit a balloon. Play with a ball.

/d/ Play with a toy duck, doll, dinosaur. Look at pictures of Dad.

/f/ Play with a football. Make a fan, and fan yourself. Go fishing.

/g/ Gallop like a horse. Play with cars in a toy garage. Play a game in which you give your child directions such as "stop" and "go."

/h/ Wear a hat. Make hearts for Valentine's Day. Go for a horsy ride. Play with a toy horse.

/j/ Play jumping games. Eat jellybeans.

/k/ Look for living cats or cats in pictures, toy keys, plastic cups. Bake a cake, cookies, or cupcakes with your child.

/l/ Sing "la-la-la" to the melody of a favorite song. Lick a lollipop. Find colorful leaves in the fall.

/m/ Eat a favorite food and say, "Mmm." Look at pictures of Mom.

/n/ Talk about noses. Make a necklace of pasta pieces or beads. Take a nap. Ask your child questions that have "no" answers, such as, "Are you a giraffe?"

/p/ Blow bubbles and say, "Pop!" Play with a boat, and say, "Putt-putt." Play with Play-Doh.

/r/ Eat raisins. Run around the yard. Play with a racecar, rabbit, rocket.

/s/ Pretend you are a snake and make hissing sounds. Talk about socks.

/t/ Play with a toy clock and say, "Tick-tock." Count your toes.

/v/ Play with a toy van. Play with toy cars and say, "Vroom."

/w/ Play with water in the bathtub. Put water in containers of different sizes. Talk about washing and windows.

/y/ Play with a yo-yo. Ask your child questions that have "yes" answers, such as, "Are you here?"

/z/ Zip and unzip a zipper. Pretend you are a bee and make buzzing sounds.

/ch/ Play with choo-choo trains. When you chop vegetables, talk about what you are doing. Eat cherries, chicken, cheese.

/sh/ Put your finger on your lips and say, "Sh-h-h," to signal quiet. Talk about shoes.

ask more questions to learn more. When asking him questions, it is better to give him limited choices, since open-ended questions may still be too difficult. For example, do not ask, "What did you do at Grandma's today?" Instead, ask him, "Did you color a picture at Grandma's today?" You can then expand on this by asking him, "When will you bring it home?" or "What did you do after you colored?"

❏ *Encourage pretend play.* When your child pushes a box across the floor and says, "Vroom," he is pretending that the box is a car. This shows that he understands symbols, or how one thing can stand for another. This skill will help him understand letters and numbers, which are also symbols.

Pretend play also helps children to develop their language skills. When your child speaks into his toy telephone or to his stuffed animals, he is practicing to talk. He is using words to live out his fantasies. Sometimes, through pretend play, children practice solving problems. Researchers believe that our ability in adulthood to think logically and devise solutions first begins to develop in childhood as we play. If your child asks you to join him in playing pretend, take the role he offers you and follow his lead. For example, if he tells you he is a dog, offer him a pretend bone.

For additional activities to help your child learn language and other skills, see Chapters 5 through 8.

Your baby has been learning the art of communicating since his first birth cry. By responding to these early attempts at communication, you have been giving him reason to communicate by teaching him that language can produce wonderful results. As we learned in this chapter, during the first three years of life, most children make tremendous strides in their ability to understand what others are saying and to express their own wants and needs.

In the next chapter, we will discuss some communication puzzlers and what to do if your child seems to be developing language skills at a slower pace than his age peers.

10

Communication Puzzlers

Your child is unique and special. When, and only when, she is ready, she will turn over, crawl across the living room, take her first step, and say her first word. Children display variation in the development of language skills, muscle coordination, and social skills, but most develop these skills within normal time limits. Most children learn to talk rather effortlessly. Therefore, it may be puzzling to parents, and even to professionals, why some children do not begin to talk within a reasonable amount of time. Many parents blame themselves as they compare their child's language development to that of their other children, their nieces or nephews, or other children in the neighborhood. This may create unnecessary pressure for the child, as well as between family members.

Nancy, mother of eighteen-month-old Josh, said that she dreads going to family picnics. This is because her niece, at seventeen months of age, is already putting two words together, while Josh primarily grunts and points, saying only a few words. Nancy's husband often asks her, "Why doesn't he talk? You're home with him all day." This type of conflict between family members is quite common.

The parents of children who talk in full sentences by the age of two often assume that their child is very intelligent, while the parents of children who say only a few words by age two may worry. Many factors affect how quickly a child develops spoken language. Furthermore, researchers have concluded that there is no evidence to suggest that children who speak early in the normal range are more intelligent than those who speak late in the normal range.

In Chapter 9, we discussed the stages of language development. It is helpful for parents to know the normal age expectations for the different language skills, and to understand that children comprehend words before they can say them. In this chapter, we will discuss some of the reasons that children deviate from the "norm," and what to do if you have any concerns about your child's development.

NORMAL VERSUS DELAYED LANGUAGE DEVELOPMENT

"Between 2 and 3, there is tremendous variability in what's normal," says Catherine Snow, PhD. Her research revealed that there are two-year-old children with vocabularies of 2,000 words and three-year-old children with vocabularies of only 150 words.

To understand development, speech/language professionals study how and when language skills develop in children. There is not much variation in the "how" because children tend to develop language skills in a certain order. For example, they usually have about 50 single words in their expressive vocabularies before they begin to put two words together. However, the "when"—that is, at what age children acquire each language skill—may vary enormously. Even experts sometimes cannot agree on what is "normal."

Since many factors can affect language learning, either slowing it down or enhancing it, children often develop at a slower or faster rate than what is expected. Because of the enormous variation in what is considered "normal," children who are not quite on schedule may not necessarily be delayed, but instead may be following their own individual timetable. However, a baby's understanding and expression of the language skills should be growing and developing on a continuous basis. There is certainly cause to be concerned if a child suddenly stops talking or doesn't seem to understand or be learning new words.

It is also important to keep in mind that speech is not the same as language. A child with a language delay may be able to say all the speech sounds clearly, but doesn't say many words or doesn't understand what other people say to her. A child with a speech problem may understand words and phrases, and use them to talk, but has trouble saying the sounds in the words correctly. Because people have difficulty understanding this child, they may assume that she knows less than she really does.

In reality, writes Naomi S. Baron, professor of linguistics at American University, Washington, DC, a child who has difficulty with speech may use the same sound to indicate several different words. For example, she may say "ma" in place of "milk," "mother," and "mug." She may understand the meanings of the words "milk," "mother," and "mug," but cannot use her tongue and lips to form the correct sounds. The listener may understand anyway, however, because of the child's use of gestures or the presence of the object to which she is referring (milk, her mother, or a mug). And, according to Professor Baron, if this child obviously uses "ma" to mean three different things, then "ma" counts as three separate words.

To roughly assess your child's language development over the months, use the following questions as a guide:

❏ Does my three-month-old child turn to the sound of my voice and other sounds?

❏ Does my eight-month-old child imitate speech sounds and use sounds to get attention?

❏ Does my eight- to twelve-month-old child look at people who talk to her, and show an interest and intention to communicate?

❏ Does my twelve- to fifteen-month-old child have a wide range of speech sounds in her babbling and jargoning? Does she express one or two meaningful words? Does she follow simple requests, such as "Look at the dog," and understand simple questions, such as "Do you want some more juice?"

❏ Does my eighteen-month-old child use at least ten words?

❏ Does my eighteen- to twenty-four-month-old child follow simple, one-step requests, such as "Please get the ball"?

❏ Does my two-year-old child have a vocabulary of fifty or more clear words or word approximations, such as "sue" for "shoe," and is she learning to join two words together? Does she ask simple questions, and respond to simple questions with "yes" and "no"?

❏ Does my two-and-a-half-year-old child understand simple stories and conversations, and use three words together, such as "my big blocks"?

❏ Does my three-year-old child ask and answer "where," "what," and "who" questions? Does she start conversations? Does she use four words and sentences to talk and make requests? Does she follow two-step directions, such as "Get the doll and put it in the box"?

Most experts agree that if your child does not meet the aforementioned conditions within reasonable time limits, you may have cause for concern.

SEEKING HELP

Many times, the parents of a child who is slow to speak hesitate to seek professional advice. Instead, they justify their child's not talking by saying, "She understands everything we say," or "She'll outgrow it," or "He's a boy." Yes, these assumptions may be true in some cases, but certainly not in all. Parents should not rely on assumptions or the fact that some children talk late but catch up. Many experts believe that children as young as twelve to eighteen months who may be language delayed should be seen by a professional. This is because they may just appear to be slow at developing language, but actually may have more severe speech or language problems. Also, a toddler who becomes frustrated because she can't speak may develop behavioral problems.

How do you know if your child is merely developing language at a slower pace and will catch up? Some researchers have found that if a child understands as much as she should for her age, uses a lot of gestures for different purposes, and understands and does more things with language at least every month, she may just be developing language at her own pace. However, researchers also suggest that if this language delay continues through the child's third year of life, there is less chance she will "outgrow" it. In addition, late-talking girls seem to have less chance for a spontaneous recovery than late-talking boys. And *some* late talkers also display one or more of the following characteristics:

❐ Show little interest in skills such as looking, pointing, and taking turns in baby games.

❐ Often sit and wait to be brought into activities with other children and adults. Sometimes, they do not seem to be aware of other people.

❐ Are self-directed and do not like to follow anyone's lead.

If you feel that your child may be a late talker, there are a number of activities you can do with her that may give her language development a boost. For a sampling of these activities, see Chapters 4 through 9. In addition, you can take your child to a speech/language pathologist. Speech/language pathologists are trained to evaluate and treat children and adults with speech or language problems. For children, they administer tests that show how much language is understood (receptive language) and how much can be said (expressive language). They may also listen to how the child speaks in different settings, and determine why she may be slow to develop language. With this information in hand, they can then offer suggestions for stimulating language development or suggest more formal treatment programs. If your child is a late talker, taking her to a speech/language pathologist may help you to achieve peace of mind when you learn that your child is developing normally, or get your child needed help and possibly avoid future learning and/or behavioral problems. For assistance with finding a speech/language pathologist, see "What Is a Speech/Language Pathologist?" on page 92.

RED FLAGS

Although still somewhat puzzled, professionals now have a better understanding of why some children do not develop language skills as quickly as others. Some of these possible causes are:

❐ Being born "at risk" or with an underlying condition.

❐ Having a family history of speech and language problems.

❐ Being male.

❐ Having a greater desire to be active than to talk.

❐ Being born the second or later child.

❐ Having frequent ear infections.

❐ Having developmental delays.

❐ Not having adequate language stimulation.

❐ Not having reasons or opportunities to communicate with others.

The following story of Joey illustrates a few of the reasons why children who were not born at risk may not talk as well as their peers. At-risk, or high-risk, children are in danger of experiencing a substantial developmental delay if not provided with early intervention services. The flags next to the "About Joey" boxes indicate whether the factors discussed are possible causes of Joey's language delay. The black flags indicate that the factors are possible causes, and the white flags indicate that they are not.

What Is a Speech/Language Pathologist?

A speech/language pathologist is a professional who is trained to diagnose and treat a variety of conditions that interfere with the ability to communicate effectively. They treat both children and adults. When choosing a speech/language pathologist, make sure he or she has the American Speech-Language-Hearing Association's Certificate of Clinical Competence. Professionals who have this certificate display the initials "CCC" after their name. The certificate indicates that the professional holds either a master's degree or a doctorate degree, has met specific requirements in course work, has had supervised professional experience, has passed a national exam, and abides by the American Speech-Language-Hearing Association's Code of Ethics. The professional may also be licensed by the state.

When interviewing speech/language pathologists, ask the following important questions:

❒ What age groups do you work with?

❒ Do you specialize in one area of difficulty, such as speech, language, or hearing?

❒ How soon could you see my child for an evaluation?

❒ Once you have evaluated my child, how long must we wait for treatment if she needs it?

❒ Does my child need to be referred to your program by a particular source, such as a physician or community agency?

❒ Once my child has been evaluated, will you be able to anticipate the length of time it will take to treat her problem?

❒ How much do you charge for evaluations and for therapy?

❒ Do you accept my insurance? Will my insurance cover the evaluation? How much of the treatment will it cover?

❒ If you cannot work with my child, can you suggest someone else for me to contact?

Speech/language pathologists can be found at school, college, and university clinics; at hospital clinics; and in private practice. To find a speech/language pathologist near you, contact the American Speech-Language-Hearing Association (ASHA) at 10801 Rockville Pike, Rockville, Maryland 20852; 800–638–8255 or 301–897–8662 (voice or TTY). E-mail can be sent to ASHA at irc@asha.org (e-mail), and the organization's website can be found at http//www.asha.org/index.htm.

Meet Joey

Joey is a happy, healthy twenty-one-month-old boy. His family includes his mother and father, both of whom are full-time professionals, and a sister, Mary, age thirty-eight months. Joey arrived in the speech/language pathologist's office held by his dad, who also held Mary's hand. Dad described with pride how Mary had heard a newscast on the ride over that had said a thunderstorm was coming that night. He said Mary had quickly exclaimed, "I don't like thunder! It scares me!"

In a confused, sad manner, he next described Joey. While Mary had spoken in complete sentences by the age of two years, Joey, who was only three months away from his second birthday, was still using very few words to communicate.

"He understands everything we say," Dad said. "I know he's smart, but he calls everything a 'ba,' even Mommy. I'm not sure if Mary was just an early talker and we're overreacting. There was a child at the babysitter's who didn't speak until he was three, and now, at age four, is talking fine. Is Joey just being stubborn, or is it because he's a boy? He just doesn't seem to be getting any better with talking. I haven't seen a change in his talking in many months."

Family Background

Many grandparents have uttered the words, "Don't worry! His father did not talk until he was three."

Research tells us not to ignore this insight because it may be important. Studies have shown that at least some aspects of language development are hereditary. If a parent was slow to talk, the biological child may be slow to talk, too.

 ABOUT JOEY

Joey's parents were not late talkers.

Gender and Personality

How many times have your heard, "He's a boy. He'll outgrow it."

Experts disagree over whether gender plays a role, but most say that if gender does, it is less than most people think. Girls tend to outpace boys verbally by only one or two months. Many researchers feel this is not because of earlier brain development, but simply because parents tend to talk more to girls and be more physical with boys. One study found that American mothers, for no apparent reason, actually talk more to their infant daughters than to their infant sons. Also, children who are very active physically may develop language later than their peers. Boys, who are generally more active than girls, sometimes develop movement first, then focus on language, rather than developing both skills at the same time. According to Dr. Snow, early talkers tend to be girls, while very late talkers tend to be boys.

 ABOUT JOEY

Joey is a very active boy. His motor skills appear to be well developed, as he walked before his first birthday. He loves to be outdoors and especially enjoys climbing on the swing set in the backyard.

Birth Order

A child's birth order may affect her ability to understand and express words. This is because, if the child is an "only child," she will naturally get all of her parents' attention. If she has siblings, she must share her parents' attention.

Naomi Baron suggested that first-born and later-born children actually have different styles of talking. First-born children use many words that name things, such as "dog," "hat," and "shoe." They pick up these words fast and say them clearly. They often put two words together readily. Later-born children, Professor Baron said, are slower to talk and don't speak as clearly. Their first words usually are not words that name things, but more likely words that adults use often in social interactions, such as "please," "thank you," and "bye-bye."

Judith Becker Bryand, PhD, noted that an older sibling talking to a younger sibling in a playful way might encourage language development. However, researchers agree that an older sibling consistently talking "for" a younger sibling may decrease the younger child's desire to talk. Think about it: Mom isn't watching when Joey points to the juice on the table. To help her younger brother, Mary quickly intervenes, saying, "Mom, Joey wants more juice." Mom gets the juice for Joey. Joey's need is met, and he never had to say a word.

 ABOUT JOEY

Joey is the second child. His older sister speaks clearly, and often relays Joey's needs and wants to their mother, father, or babysitter.

History of Ear Infections

In the United States, ear infections account for 30 million doctor visits each year, placing them second to the common cold as the most common health problem among preschool children. About 50 percent of children have at least one ear infection by their first birthday. "Otitis media" is the medical term for a middle ear infection. It usually involves inflammation and/or buildup of fluid in the area behind the eardrum, which is the middle ear. Most ear infections occur between the ages of four months and three years, when children are listening and learning to talk.

Because a young child's eustachian tube, the passage that connects the middle ear to the throat, is shorter and straighter than that of an adult, germs can easily travel there. When the middle ear is filled with fluid, the three tiny bones in the middle ear that carry the sound vibrations from the eardrum to the inner ear cannot transmit the sounds as well as they should. This may result in a temporary mild or moderate hearing loss. This is why, when children have an ear infection, the sounds they hear are not clear and precise. Plug your ears with your fingers, and listen to someone talk. This is how voices sound to children with ear infections.

If a child has frequent ear infections, the result may be damage to the eardrum, which may cause permanent hearing loss. If fluid from an infection remains in the ear without treatment, a child may develop speech or language problems that continue through her school years. Even a temporary mild hearing loss from an ear infection can slow a child's ability to understand language and, thus, to speak. However, with early intervention, serious medical complications usually can be controlled.

The symptoms, severity, and length of ear infections vary. Often, a child may have fluid in the ear that affects her hearing, but no signs of fever or pain. Sometimes, weeks or months may pass before a parent realizes the child has an infection. To determine if your child has an ear infection, check for the following symptoms:

❏ *Nonresponsiveness to sounds.* Your child may closely watch your face or pull your face toward her when you speak to her. She may not respond when called from another room.

❏ *Earache or draining from the ear.* The discharge may be thin and watery, or thick with mucus.

❏ *Lethargy, irritability, or crankiness.* Your child may suddenly seem to become lethargic or uninterested in her surroundings. She may be unusually irritable or cranky.

❏ *Unusual clumsiness.* Your child may fall down or bump into things more often than usual.

❏ *Fever, headache, vomiting, disturbed sleep, and/or no appetite.* Your child may display one or any combination of these symptoms.

❏ *Rubbing, pulling, or scratching the ears.*

❏ *Decreased amount of verbalization.*

❏ *Unclear or mumbled speech.*

If you suspect that your child has an ear infection, call your pediatrician immediately. The doctor may prescribe medication to help clear up the infection. If your child does have an ear infection, remember to take her back to the doctor for a follow-up visit to make sure her hearing has returned to normal.

In addition to obtaining medical treatment, there are other measures you can take. You can compensate for your child's temporary hearing loss by talking louder than usual. In addition, when you read to you child, point to pictures as you read their names. Doing this will provide visual clues as well as auditory clues to make your message clear. It will help your child better understand the words you are saying.

 ABOUT JOEY

Joey has had only a few detected ear infections. These were at approximately six to eight months of age. Each time, he was treated with antibiotics and re-checked by his pediatrician to make sure the infection had completely cleared.

Developmental Progress

Babies develop on a daily basis. In addition to learning new methods of communication, they also learn new ways to move their muscles, to think, and to relate to people. All these skills are expected to develop at certain times in life. A child who is developmentally delayed may be behind his age peers in many areas, including:

☐ Physical motor development—refers to the way a child's muscles work and her body develops.

☐ Cognitive development—refers to the way a child's brain makes sense out of what she hears, sees, tastes, smells, or touches; the way her brain thinks.

☐ Social/emotional development—refers to the way a child manages her emotions and relates to other people and to her environment.

☐ Language development—refers to the way a child learns to understand others and to express her own thoughts and ideas.

A child who is developmentally delayed may be late to talk, as well as display problems in any of the other areas of development. Talking late may not be an isolated symptom or problem.

 ABOUT JOEY

Joey's pediatrician has concluded that he is developing normally in all areas except language.

Language Stimulation

As discussed in previous chapters, babies learn to talk by listening to their parents and other people talking to them. Language development depends a great deal on environmental stimulation. Research has concluded that the amount and kind of language children hear can slow down or accelerate their speech and language learning. Children who are not stimulated by being talked to may develop language at a slower pace.

ABOUT JOEY

Joey goes to a babysitter five days a week, for seven hours a day. In addition to Joey, the babysitter watches three children under the age of four years, one of whom is Joey's sister. Joey's mother describes the caregiver as a quiet, rather passive woman. The children often watch videos and television.

In the morning, while Mom and Dad get ready for work, Joey often watches a video to keep him entertained. To save Mom and Dad time, the babysitter many times dresses and feeds him. During the car ride to the babysitter's house, Mom will silently plan her day or talk to Mary about the evening's plans.

After work, Mom generally does her errands before she picks up Joey and Mary. Once at home, the children may play alone in the yard or watch television while she prepares dinner and does her household chores. When Dad arrives home, he usually plays physical games with the children before dinner. Mom talks to the children while she bathes them and gets them ready for bed, but she admits that she is often preoccupied with work she has brought home to do after the children are asleep. Joey listens to bedtime stories for about two minutes, then usually leaves Mom's lap to play alone with a toy while Mary continues to listen. Joey doesn't seem to listen while he plays.

On the weekend, Mom tends to leave Joey at home, napping with Dad, while she and Mary go to the grocery store or do other errands around town.

Treatment and Result

Joey's parents' concerns prompted them to see a speech/language pathologist for an evaluation. This was a wise decision for many reasons. Even though they knew that Joey was behind his age peers, they weren't sure what he should be doing. Also, he didn't seem to be progressing—that is, understanding and learning new words.

Joey's parents have become more aware of the time they spend talking and interacting (or *not* talking and interacting) with Joey. They have learned to utilize their daily routine activities to help Joey learn language. Bathing, dressing, eating breakfast, and riding in the car have become valuable language-learning times. Joey now also often accompanies his mother on errands to places such as the supermarket and post office. In addition, his caretaker uses the five methods of language stimulation. She has found that as he learns to tell her his needs and wants, he is becoming more independent and happy.

Every child is unique and special, and will develop language skills when ready. If you are concerned about your child, it is important that you not rely on your impressions of what she should be doing, but learn what "normal" children do at certain ages. Of course, guidelines are just guidelines. If you have any questions or concerns about your child's development in any area, your wisest move would be to seek professional guidance. A licensed speech/language professional will address your concerns about your child's speech and language development. In addition, you should also keep an eye on your child's hearing by taking her to the pediatrician if you suspect an ear infection.

Removing needless worry about your child's development, as well as getting assistance for realistic problems, can make you more relaxed and ready to enjoy the fun of helping your baby learn to talk.

Appendix A

Parent Worksheet

Think about an activity your child enjoys. Use this worksheet to explore ways in which you can use the activity to enhance your child's language learning. Jot down what you see, do, think, and feel during the activity.

Activity: _____

1. Naming _____

Word labels (names of items): _____

_____

_____

Categories (names of groups of items): _____

_____

_____

2. Describing _____

Colors (red, blue, green): _____

_____

_____

Shapes (round, square, triangular):_____

_____

_____

Textures (how items feel):_____

_____

_____

Quantities (how many or how much):_____

_____

_____

3. Comparing ─────────────────────────────

Opposites (old/new, up/down, high/low): _____

_____

_____

Sizes (big, bigger, biggest): _____

_____

_____

4. Explaining ─────────────────────────────

Logical order of events (first/next, before/after): _____

_____

_____

Things that go together (bed/sheets, pail/shovel):_____

_____

_____

Action words (run, jump, splash):_____

_____

_____

5. Giving Directions ──────────────────────

Spatial awareness (up, between, under):_____

_____

_____

Appendix B

Resources for Parents and Caregivers

Federal Assistance and Support

Child Care Bureau
U.S. Department of Health and
   Human Services
Administration for Children and
   Families
Office of Public Affairs
370 L'Enfant Promenade, SW
Washington, DC 20202

Corporation for National Service
Training and Technical Assistance
Room 4821
1201 New York Avenue, NW
Washington, DC 20595

Even Start
U.S. Department of Education
Compensatory Education Programs
Office of Elementary and Secondary
   Education
600 Independence Avenue, SW
Room 4400
Portals Building
Washington, DC 20202-6132

Head Start
U.S. Department of Health and
   Human Services
Administration for Children
   and Families
Office of Public Affairs
370 L'Enfant Promenade, SW
Washington, DC 20202

National Information Center for
   Children and Youth With
   Disabilities
P.O. Box 1492
Washington, DC 20013

National Institute of Child Health
   and Human Development
U.S. Department of Health and
   Human Services
National Institutes of Child Health
Building 31, Room 2A32, MSC-2425
31 Center Drive
Bethesda, MD 20842-2425

Office of Special Education
  Programs
U.S. Department of Education
600 Independence Avenue, SW
Switzer Building
Room 4613
Washington, DC 20202

Title I
U.S. Department of Education
Compensatory Education Programs
Office of Elementary and Secondary
  Education
600 Independence Avenue, SW
Room 4400
Portals Building
Washington, DC 20202-6132

Organizations

Alliance for Technology Access
2175 East Francisco Boulevard
Suite L
San Rafael, CA 94901
415–455–4575

American Speech-Language-Hearing
  Association (ASHA)
10801 Rockville Pike
Rockville, MD 20852
301–897–700 (voice and TTY)
800–638–8255 (toll-free)
E-mail: webmaster@asha.org
Website:
  http://www.asha.org/index.htm

Cleft Palate Foundation
1218 Grandview Avenue
Pittsburgh, PA 15211
412–481–1376
800–242–5338 (toll-free)
Website: http://www.cleft.com

Council for Exceptional Children
  (CEC)
Division for Children With
  Communication Disorders
1920 Association Drive
Reston, VA 22091-1589
703–620–3660
Website: http://www.cec.sped.org

National Down Syndrome Congress
National Center
1605 Chantilly Drive
Suite 250
Atlanta, GA 30324
404–633–1555
800–232–NDSC (toll-free)

National Easter Seal Society
230 West Monroe Street
Suite 1800
Chicago, IL 60606-4802
312–726–6200
312–726–4258 (TTY)
800–221–6827 (toll-free)
E-mail: nassinfo@seals.com
Website: http://www.seals.com

Scottish Rite Foundation
Southern Jurisdiction, USA, Inc.
1733 Sixteenth Street, NW
Washington, DC 20009-3199
202–232–3579

Trace Research and Development
  Center
University of Wisconsin-Madison
S-151 Waisman Center
Madison, WI 53705-2280
608–262–6966
609–263–5408 (TTY)

Telephone Help

Child Care Aware
800–424–2246 (toll-free)
Referrals to licensed and accredited childcare centers. Also provides a free packet of information on how to choose quality child care. Coordinated by the National Association of Child Care Resource and Referral Agencies. Weekdays, 9 AM to 5 PM (CST).

ChildHelp National Hotline
800–443–7237
Twenty-four-hour advice and referrals for children and adults with questions or in a crisis.

National Parent Information
Network
800–583–4135
Referrals, abstracts, and answers from researchers free of charge. Weekdays, 8 AM to 4:30 PM (PST).

Single Parents Association
800–704–2102
Referrals to local support groups and community resources. Also, fields questions on parenting skills. Weekdays, 9 AM to 6 PM (CST).

Websites

Childbirth.Org
http://www.childbirth.org
Top discussion forums and a home page with answers to tough questions.

Family.com
http://www.family.com
A Disney site. Bulletin board and chat rooms with voices of intelligent and caring parents.

ParenTalk Newsletter
http://www.tnpc.com/parentalk/
    index.html
Clearly written articles by physicians and psychologists.

ParenthoodWeb
http://parenthoodweb.com
Pediatricians and psychiatrists respond to e-mail. Also, immediate answers to stock questions.

Parenting Q&A
http://parenting-qa.com
Essays, reading lists, and games for rainy days.

Zero to Three
http://www.zerotothree.org
Discussion forums.

Parent
Glossary

At risk. Refers to a child less than three years of age who is in danger of experiencing a substantial developmental delay if not provided with early intervention services. Also called *high risk.*

Auditory discrimination. The ability to hear the differences in sounds.

Babbling. Vocal play; the sounds that babies make when they combine a consonant and vowel, and repeat the same syllable over and over again. Examples are "baba" and "gagaga."

Cause and effect. The concept that every action has a result or consequence.

Cognitive development. Refers to the way a child's brain makes sense out of what he hears, sees, tastes, smells, and touches; the way his brain thinks.

Communication. The exchange of thoughts or messages using speech, symbols, or writing.

Concept word. A word describing a general idea or characteristic such as position (in, on, under), time (first, before, after), quality (big, old, cold), and quantity (more, some, one).

Consonants. The letters whose sounds we make by restricting our outgoing breath. The consonants of the English language include "b," "k," "p," "s," and "z."

Developmentally delayed. When a child's development of physical motor, cognitive, language, or social/emotional skills is slower than what is considered normal for his age group.

Eustachian tube. The passage that connects the middle ear to the throat.

Expansion. The technique of repeating what your child says and expanding it by adding one or two words.

Expansion plus. The technique of repeating what your child says and expanding it by adding the appropriate grammar and an additional sentence or two.

Expressive language. The language used to express thoughts and feelings, answer questions, and relate events. It includes words, tone of voice, gestures, and rate of speech.

Generalization. The recognition of similar attributes shared by different items.

Grammar. The rules of a language that determine how its words are combined into sentences.

Intelligence quotient (IQ). A measurement of learning ability and achievement.

Jargon. The early true language sounds that children make by putting vowels and consonants together, and using real tone and inflection. An example is "bagada."

Language. A set of symbols used by people to communicate. These symbols can be written, spoken, or gestural.

Language development. Refers to the way a child learns to understand others and to express his own thoughts and ideas.

Language disorder. A noticeable problem with understanding and/or expressing thoughts and ideas.

Linguist. A person who is skilled in languages.

Means to an end. The concept that you plan a course of action to accomplish a goal.

Middle ear. The portion of the ear that transmits sound. It is located between the outer ear and the inner ear, and includes the eardrum, three tiny bones (malleus, incus, and stapes), the facial nerve, and the eustachian tube.

Modeling. Providing examples of acceptable verbal responses.

Neuron. A nerve cell in the brain.

Normal development. What the experts agree most children do at certain ages.

Object permanence. The concept that an object continues to exist even though you can't see it.

Otitis media. The medical term for when fluid is present in the middle ear.

Parallel talk. The technique of talking out loud about what your child is seeing, feeling, hearing, and touching at that moment.

Parentese. The special way in which people all over the world speak to infants and toddlers. It may include a higher pitch, short utterances, repetition, and substitution of proper nouns for pronouns ("Mommy has it" instead of "I have it").

Physical motor development. Refers to the way a child's muscles work and body develops.

Receptive language. The language that is understood when read, heard, or seen.

Self-talk. The technique of talking out loud about what you are seeing, feeling, hearing, and touching at the moment.

Social/emotional development. Refers to the way a child relates to other people and to the environment.

Speech. The sounds made when communicating a message verbally.

Speech/language pathologist. A person who is qualified to diagnose and treat children and adults with communication problems.

Universal grammar. Fundamental rules of grammar common to all languages.

Visual discrimination. The ability to recognize how items are the same and different.

Vocabulary. The words you know. Your receptive vocabulary consists of the words you understand. Your expressive vocabulary consists of the words you are able to use to express yourself.

Vocal play. The pre-speech sounds that babies make as they experiment with their voices.

Vowels. The letters whose sounds we make when air passes through our nose and mouth without friction or stoppage. The vowels of the English language are "a," "e," "i," "o," and "u."

Bibliography

Books

Adler, Irving, and Joyce Adler. *Language and Man.* New York: John Day Co., 1970.

America Reads Challenge: Ready Set Read for Caregivers: Early Childhood Language Activities for Children From Birth Through Age Five. Washington, DC: Corporation for National Service, U.S. Department of Education, and U.S. Department of Health and Human Services, 1997.

Blank, Marion, and M. Ann Marquis. *Directing Discourse.* Tucson, AZ: Communication Skill Builders, 1987.

Bolle, Edmund Blair. *So Much to Say.* New York: St. Martin's Press, 1992.

DeFeo, Anthony B. *Parent Articles 2.* Tucson, AZ: Communication Skill Builders, 1995.

Fowler, William. *Talking From Infancy.* Cambridge, MA: Brookline Books, 1990.

Kumin, Libby. *Communication Skills in Children With Down Syndrome: A Guide for Parents.* Rockville, MD: Woodbine House, 1994.

Mohr, Merilyn. *Home Playgrounds.* Ontario: Camden House Publishing, 1987.

Schrader, Margaret. *Parent Articles.* Tucson, AZ: Communication Skill Builders, 1988.

Schwartz, Sue, and Joan E. Heller Miller. *The Language of Toys.* Rockville, MD: Woodbine House, 1988.

Swisher, Clause. *The Beginning of Language.* San Diego, CA: Green Haven Press, Inc., 1989.

Thomas, Linda. *Beginning Syntax.* Cambridge, MA: Blackwell Publishers, 1993.

Wallach, Geraldine P., and Lynda Miller. *Language Intervention and Academic Success.* Boston: Little, Brown and Co., 1987.

Weybright, Glenn, and Jo Rosenthal Tanzer. *Putting It Into Words.* Tucson, AZ: Communication Skill Builders, 1985.

Periodicals

Allman, William F. "The Clues in Idle Chatter: From Babies' Babbling to Baseball Commentary: Nuances of Everyday Conversation Offer Insights Into How the Brain Learns the Complexities of Language." *U.S. News and World Report,* Vol. 111, No. 8 (19 August 1991), pp. 61–63.

Begley, Sharon. "Your Child's Brain." *Newsweek,* Vol. 127, No. 8 (19 February 1996), pp. 54–61.

Begley, Sharon, and Pat Wingert. "Teach Your Parents Well: As Research Unlocks the Secrets of Babies' Brains, Families Have a Hard Time Learning the Lessons." *Newsweek,* Vol. 129, No. 17 (28 April 1997), pp. 72–73.

Bower, Bruce. "Talkative Parents Make Kids Smarter." *Science News,* Vol. 150 (17 August 1996), pp. 100–101.

Brownlee, Shannon. "Baby Talk." *U.S. News and World Report,* 15 June 1998, pp. 48–54.

Fisch, Robert O.; Marty Smith; and Margaret Yatsevitch Phinney. "Project Read—The Importance of Early Learning." *American Family Physician,* Vol. 56, No. 9 (December 1997), pp. 215–218.

Frost, Joe L. "Child Development and Playgrounds." *Parks and Recreation,* Vol. 32, No. 4 (April 1997), pp. 54–61.

Gleitman, Lila R. "A Human Universal: The Capacity to Learn a Language." *Modern Philology,* Vol 90, No. 4 (May 1993), pp. 13–34.

Gertner, Bethany L.; Mabel L. Rice; and Pamela A. Hadley. "Influence of Communicative Competence on Peer Preferences in a Preschool Classroom." *Journal of Speech and Hearing Research,* Vol. 37, No. 4 (August 1994), pp. 913–924.

Graeber, Laurel. "Raising Smart Kids." *Parents Magazine,* May 1998.

Helms, Ann Doris. "Talk, Talk, More Talk: It's the Elixir of Growth." Knight-Ridder/Tribune News Service, 15 April 1997, pg. 415K7699.

Henderson, Sally J.; Nancy Ewald Jackson; and Reisa A. Mukamal. "Early Development of Language and Literacy Skills of an Extremely Precocious Reader." *Gifted Child Quarterly,* Vol. 37, No. 2 (Spring 1993), pp. 78–84.

Huttenlocher, Janellen; Wendy Haight; Anthony Bryk; Michael Seltzer; and Thomas Lyons. "Early Vocabulary Growth: Relation to Language Input and Gender." *Developmental Psychology,* Vol. 27, No. 2 (1991), pp. 236–248.

Jusczyk, Peter W., and Elizabeth A. Hohne. "Infant's Memory for Spoken Words." *Science,* Vol. 277, No. 5334 (26 September 1997), pp. 1984–1987.

"Knowing Isn't Saying: Early Receptive Language Abilities." *The Brown University Child and Adolescent Behavior Letter,* Vol. 12, No. 11 (November 1996), pp. 1–4.

Laliberte, Richard. "Parents Report." *Parents Magazine,* September 1997, pp. 49–56.

Long, Katherine. "Infant Learning Starts Early, Research Shows." *Philadelphia Inquirer,* 20 May 1997.

Menyuk, Paula; Marie Chesnick; Jacqueline Weis Liebergott; Blanche Korngold; Ralph D. Agostino; and Albert Belanger. "Predicting Reading Problems in At-Risk Children." *Journal of Speech and Hearing Research,* Vol. 34, No. 4 (August 1991): pp. 893–904.

Monaco, Anthony. "Research Links Gene to Language Development." *The New York Times,* 27 January 1998, pg. F8.

Nash, J. Madeleine. "How a Child's Brain Develops: Fertile Minds." *Time,* February 1997, pp. 49–52.

Paul, Rhea, and Terril J. Elwood. "Maternal Linguistic Input to Toddlers With Slow Expressive Language Development." *Journal of Speech and Hearing Research,* Vol. 34, No. 5 (October 1991), pp. 982–989.

Paul, Rhea; Shawn Spangle Looney, and Pamela S. Dahm. "Communication and Socialization Skills at Ages 2 and 3 in 'Late Talking' Young Children." *Journal of Speech and Hearing Research,* Vol. 34, No. 4 (August 1991), pp. 858–866.

Ramey, Sharon Landesman, and Craig T. Ramey. "The Transition to School: Why the First Few Years Matter for a Lifetime." *Phi Delta Kappan,* Vol. 7, No. 3 (November 1994), pp. 194–199.

Rosenberg, Sheldon. "Chomsky's Theory of Language: Some Recent Observations." *Psychological Science,* Vol. 4, No. 1 (January 1993), pp. 15–20.

Rossetti, Louis M. "Happy Talking: Understanding and Promoting a Child's Communication." *The Exceptional Parent,* Vol. 27, No. 2 (February 1997), pp. 22–24.

Sharpe, Rochelle. "To Boost IQ's, Aid Is Needed in First 3 Years." *The Wall Street Journal,* 12 April 1994, pp. B1, B10.

"Suggestions for Stimulating Speech Sounds." *Communicating Together,* Vol. 11, No. 5 (January/February 1995), pg. 5.

Whitehurse, Grover J., and Janet E. Fischel. "Practitioner Review: Early Developmental Language Delay: What, If Anything, Should the Clinician Do About It?" *Journal of Child Psychology and Psychiatry and Allied Disciplines,* Vol. 35, No. 4 (May 1994), pp. 613–649.

Index